Tracking Touri

Movement and mobility

Anne Hardy

(G) **Goodfellow Publishers Ltd**

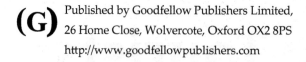

Published by Goodfellow Publishers Limited,
26 Home Close, Wolvercote, Oxford OX2 8PS
http://www.goodfellowpublishers.com

British Library Cataloguing in Publication Data: a catalogue record for this title is available from the British Library.

Library of Congress Catalog Card Number: on file.

ISBN: 978-1-911635-39-0

DOI: 110.23912/9781911635383-4277

 Design and typesetting by P.K. McBride, www.macbride.org.uk

Cover design by Cylinder

Printed by Marston Book Services, www.marston.co.uk

Contents

Dedication

This book is dedicated to my parents, Robert and Elaine Hardy,
who have never stopped questioning and innovating.
And for those gifts, I am truly thankful.

Foreword

Many years ago, when I was working at the University of Northern British Columbia, a colleague and I were discussing the mobility of recreational vehicle users (RVers) on the Alaska Highway. We noted that while research had explored their socio-demographic status and length of trip, almost nothing was known about their travel itineraries. No one really knew where these tourists went. This thought stayed with me until 2015 when I was living in Tasmania and an opportunity arose to apply for research that used technology to assist the tourism industry. I recalled this data dearth, applied for research funding through Sense-T and one year later Tourism Tracer was born.

Tourism Tracer is a bespoke research app that tracks tourists for their entire journey using GPS technology, and syncs this with their socio-demographic and travel experience data. The app and data dashboard drew the attention of many tourism industry bodies who enjoyed its ability to collect data and visualise it in close to real time. It was suggested that the app was one of the first of its type to track tourists for their entire journey through an entire destination, with their consent. Tourism Tracer gained so much attention that myself and my research team were suddenly thrust into many new research and industry realms – the tourist tracking research world, the innovation world, the pitching world and when interest came from potential investors, the commercial world. It challenged the way we thought about collecting, analysing, visualising data, and as time has progressed, it has also challenged the way we think about how tourists travel.

But in addition to the accolades, Tourism Tracer challenged us as researchers. Technology is a difficult beast to tame. When you combine research and technology with tourists, there are many things that can go wrong. And I have experienced this on many, many occasions! App technology can fail, mobile networks can fail, phones can fail, and tourists can so 'no' when asked to participate in this form of research. Moreover, new technologies can emerge which challenge existing ones and in differing contexts, can perform better than their predecessors.

Almost all the technologies and methods for tracking tourists that are detailed in this book did not exist twenty years ago. More significantly, for tourism researchers, research using these new technologies is scarce at best and disparate at worst. I am constantly being asked to compare methods and find that their strengths often differ, depending on the research question, context, research team and project circumstances such as budget and time. I am also constantly being asked about the ethics of tracking tourists' mobility.

This book is designed to try and bridge these gaps. It is designed to assist those who wish to learn about different tourist tracking methods and compare their relative pros and cons, plus consider the ethical considerations that these methods demand. While technological change is imminent and is constantly discussed openly, I find that there is increasing concern about the ethics of these methods. This book seeks to tackle this issue head-on by assessing the relative strengths and weakness of each method, both in terms of its ability to collect data and its ability to be applied in an ethical manner.

The development of Tourism Tracer and my interest in tracking tourists' mobility was not a solo endeavour – there are many people who were behind the inception of Tourism Tracer and my research into tourist tracking. I am truly grateful for their input. In particular, I thank those involved in the design of Tourism Tracer. I thank my co-lead Richard Eccleston and project manager, Sarah Hyslop. I also thank the rest of the Tourism Tracer team- Jagannath Aryal, Brady Robards, Dugald Tinch, Kate Booth and Tommy Wong, plus Ulrike Gretzel, Bob McKercher, Dan Wang, Amit Birenboim and Noam Shoval. I also thank Bruna Silva Ragaini, Martha Wells and Elleke Leurs for their involvement in our data analysis and recruitment. I would also like to thank Ruth Steel from the University of Tasmania, plus the business development team for their ongoing support, plus the staff from our research office who have so patiently assisted me with my tracking research. Importantly I thank our industry partners: Gulliver and Ionata, who created the wonderful technology for us, and our funders: Sense T, the Tasmanian government, the Tourism Industry Council of Tasmania, the Federal Group and the four regional tourism organisations who funded early tranches of Tourism Tracer. I also wish to pass my very warm and special thanks to Sally North from Goodfellow for approaching me and putting her faith in me when asking me to prepare this manuscript. And finally, I thank Alice, Peter and Hannah who have always supported me, particularly as I have prepared this book.

I hope you enjoy it.

Anne 14/9/2020

About the author

Anne Hardy is an Associate Professor in Tourism and Society and Co-Director of the Tourism Research and Education Network (TRENd), at the University of Tasmania, Australia. Anne grew up in Tasmania, undertook her PhD at the University of Queensland, and worked at the University of Northern British Columbia before returning to Tasmania. She is currently interested in three research areas: tourism and social justice; sustainable tourism; and understanding tourist behaviour via technology. Anne leads the Tourism Tracer project (www.tourismtracer.com) that has received international acclaim, won numerous awards and has recently been commercialised. Her research has been published widely in academic journals, books and via the media. Her approach to research seeks to extend knowledge in a two-way direction between the tourism industry and academia.

1 Introduction

What this chapter will cover:

- Early methods of wayfinding.
- Early evidence of mobility and tourism.
- Early evidence recording tourists' movement.
- The genesis of modern travel and technology.
- Recent technological innovations and big data.
- The mobility paradigm and new mobility paradigm.

Introduction

In the past twenty years we have seen changes in technology that have reconfigured the way in which tourists plan, travel, reflect and share experiences. These changes have caused us to reconsider how tourists travel and how they make decisions, as well as how destinations market themselves. The now ubiquitous use of mobile phones has been documented as being a major influence (Wang, Park and Fesenmaier, 2012). Yet, while large swathes of research have focused on the use of technology and the impact that technology has had upon tourists' decision making, there is comparatively far less research that concentrates on using technology to understand where tourists travel to, and how they move between destinations and attractions. The tourism industry has been documented as lagging far further behind than other industries in its use of technology, particularly that which delivers research insights

(Eccleston, Hardy and Hyslop, 2020). The reasons for this have not yet been explored in great detail, but they are quite possibly due to the fact that the tourism industry is dominated by small to medium sized businesses whose capacity for expenditure on the use of technology and research is limited, relative to other industry sectors such as mining and forestry. A second reason is that tourism is reliant on an element that is often far harder to control – people. Unlike sectors that use biological elements as their key resources, and can place sensors where needed without requiring consent, tourism's reliance on humans and their interaction with technology makes tracking far more complex. A third reason is that tourism arguably lags behind other sectors because the methods available to the industry to track and understand mobility involve complex technology, and different methods require specialist analytical skills. The Director General of the World Health Organisation, Tedros Adhanom Ghebreyesus, argued that decision makers are facing an 'infodemic' as a result of large swathes of data being made available in order to assist understanding the impacts of the COVID-19 pandemic (Zarocostas, 2020). The plethora of options facing the industry in regards to which technology to use and how, is undoubtedly adding to this lag.

This book seeks to assist the tourism research community by providing a review of the range of tracking methods available to researchers. Currently the broader body of work remains disparate; journal articles tend to focus on one method at a time and are published in their different disciplines. Consequently, the relative opportunities and challenges of each method have rarely been discussed side by side. In order to address this dearth, this book will devote an entire chapter to a different type of method and reviews its functions, the conceptual and methodological advances that have emerged from the application of the technique, the ethical implications of applying the technique, and its pros and cons. The book does not explain the precise methods required to analyse data using each of these methods, as an entire book could be dedicated to each chapter if this approach were to be taken. Rather, it is designed to assist researchers to choose which tracking method is most suited to their specific research needs and understand what type of technical expertise is required. The founding principle that underpins this book is that ethical research practices must occur at all times, hence the inclusion of a separate chapter that refers to this requirement and sections in each chapter that refer the ethical implications of each tracking technique.

A short history of understanding mobility and tourism

Tracking mobility is not a new phenomenon, nor one that has emerged since the advent of digital technology. There is evidence as far back as 3500 BCE that seafarers were exploring the world and tracking their location (Denny, 2012). In those times, sounding poles or lead lines were used to indicate the depth of the waters, and knowledge of winds and tides, plus the temperature and colour of water currents, was used to navigate. Celestial navigation was also used; there is evidence of Bronze Age people, the Minoans of Crete (2700 BCE to 1450 BCE), traveling from Crete to Egypt using the stars, particularly the Pole Star (Draco) to guide them. Pytheas, a Greek explorer, is also known to have used the Pole Star and possibly also a gnomon (a sundial that casts a shadow), to navigate himself in the fourth century BCE. There is also evidence of celestial navigation occurring around 3000 BCE by Taiwanese people who travelled through the islands of Southeast Asia. Polynesians, Micronesians and Melanesians were also highly skilled navigators who moved between the islands of the Pacific, using a combination of the horizon, stars and points on the horizon (Denny, 2012); a practice that still continues today.

The development of the compass had a profound impact on tracking and mobility. Its use was first recorded in China during the Qin dynasty (221–206 BCE) when the magnetic south-pointing needle was used on chariots to assist ambassadors in finding their way home. It consisted of a square slab that had markings on it for the constellations and north, south, east and west. The pointing needle was spoon-shaped and made of lodestone and would always point south (Lane, 1963; Hirth, 1906). While its existence was noted around 220 BCE, there is a dearth in the recording of this technique for several centuries after this, until 139 CE when the Chinese astronomer Chang Höng was recorded as using it it. Between 850 and 1050 CE evidence exists of magnetized needles being used in China as direction pointers, replacing the spoon-shaped lodestones. The writings of Chinese Song-dynasty scientist, Shen Gu, in 1088 CE suggested the magnetic compass had been used for many centuries prior to 1088 (Denny, 2012). It is also possible that Arabian sailors brought the compass to the west from China as there is evidence that Arabic nations were moving vast distances around the ninth century (see Hourani, *Arab Seafaring*, I09 and Taylor, *Haven-Finding*, 96 in Lane, 1963). In the twelfth century there is also evidence of its existence in in Europe and China – during this time it consisted of a magnetised needle attached to a chip floating in a bowl of water (Lane 1963). In Europe, the first recording of the use of the compass was in the thirteenth century when Europeans invented the dry compass (a needle on a pivot) around or before 1410 CE (Denny, 2012). Its use resulted in a dramatic increase in the amount of shipping in the winter months, particularly in the Mediterranean, because sailors could navigate in the dark and in poor, overcast weather, as visibility to the stars was no longer necessary. The impacts of this was visible in Mediterranean documents of the time, where charts were developed that included sailing directions (Lane, 1963).

Evidence of journeying, mobility and tourism

Developments in wayfinding techniques, along with economic and socio-political factors, facilitated the early precursors to tourism. Baines (2006) studied Ancient Greece 700-480 BCE and argued that early tourism should be considered journeying, whereby travel took place to a location some distance from where the individual lived and was undertaken for economic or migration purposes (Baines, 2006). Herodotus (484-425 BCE) is regarded by some scholars as the first 'tourist' (Feifer, 1985). He recorded his travels to Egypt in *The Histories*, which may be considered an early guidebook that assisted with decision making, wayfinding and mobility (Herodotus, 1921). His Greek compatriots are also recorded as having travelled extensively around Greece in the centuries prior to Christ's birth, for sport (Feifer, 1985).

In English texts, it is argued that the first culture to embrace mass tourism was Imperial Rome (27BCE to 476 CE) and that during the peaceful era of Pax Romana, aristocrats sought distractions from their daily lives (Feifer, 1985). During this time, travel between Hadrian's Wall and the Euphrates was relatively safe and free of borders, and an extensive network of roads, along with inns, existed between them. Consequently, the necessary tourism infrastructure existed, along with a social environment that facilitated travel. A variety of texts were developed to assist Romans with their travel plans, itinerary development, and decision making (Cioffi, 2016)). For example, the *Itinerarium Burdigalense* contained travel routes for travellers (cited in Cioffi, 2016). A popular destination was the Bay of Naples, and villas appeared in this region about 200 BCE (Feifer, 1985; Casson 1974). Following this, around 300 CE, European religious pilgrimages to places such as the Church of the Holy Sepulchre in Jerusalem became popular. In medieval times, around the early 1500s, Parks (1954) wrote, religious pilgrimages were also important to Anglo Saxon travellers who travelled between England and Rome. In the 17th century, Grand Tours of Europe became extremely popular in England amongst the aristocracy and upper classes who would travel to Europe and beyond once they had turned 21 and 'come of age' (Bates, 1911; Mead, 1914; Pimlott, 1947). The Grand Tour became a rite of passage and was supported by 'guidebooks' such as Thomas Coryat's *Coryat's Crudities* (1611), and later *An Account of Some of the Statues, Bas-Reliefs, Drawings, and Pictures in Italy* published in 1722 (Richardson, 1722). Towards the end of the 18th century, spa bathing and seaside resorts became popular amongst the upper classes, and much research has focussed on the development of seaside resorts and spas in Britain and France in the 19th century (Bukart and Medlik, 1981).

However, this western-centric view is not the sum total of evidence of the genesis of tourism and materials designed to assist with mobility. There is evidence that Chinese women have been travelling as far back as the Han dynasty (206 BCE-220 CE). This exists in the poem by Ban Zhao called *Dong Zheng Fu* that recounts Ban Zhao's journey as she followed her son who was travelling to take up an official appointment (Yang et al., 2017). Early records of travel in China also include travel that was undertaken for cross-cultural exchanges between India and

China, somewhere in the first century CE (Sen, 2001). This travel was stimulated by the spread of Buddhist texts from India and China that encouraged travel by Buddhist monks and pilgrims. These could be regarded as guidebooks as they assisted with decision making and mobility. For example, Faxian travelled in 399 from the Chinese capital of Chang'an (now called Xi'an) to religious sites in India and Sri Lanka and returned 14 years later. His travel was detailed in what could be considered an early guidebook – *A Record of the Buddhist Kingdoms* detailed the arduous nature of travel during that time, including the different Buddhist practices that he encountered (Sen, 2001).

In the last three hundred years, social change, such as the introduction of legislation that introduced public holidays during the industrial revolution in the 18th and 19th century, has transformed tourism and leisure. Tourism has changed from an activity confined to the upper classes to an activity available to the middle class (Hern, 1967; Robinson, 1976). From the 1800s technological advances such as the development of railway systems also had a major impact on leisure travel, facilitating mass scale transport from England's cities to coastal areas such as Brighton, Blackpool and Dover (Bukart and Medlik, 1981; Hern 1967). In the mid-twentieth century, further social change, along with the introduction of wide bodied aircraft, resulted in mass tourism.

Schwab (2016) argues that currently we are undergoing a fourth industrial revolution caused by technology. This era is characterised by the development of the World Wide Web, the Web 2.0 era, robotics, artificial intelligence and the internet of things (Tussyadiah, 2020). Most significantly for this book, this includes the introduction of mobile phones with internet access, which afford tourists the ability to communicate in real time with those at home, along with fellow travellers. The incorporation of Global Positioning Systems (GPS) technology into smart phones has also had a profound impact as it means tourists can now travel with technology that offers them real-time maps, live travel and transport information. These changes have had profound impacts upon the behaviour, mobility, and decision making of tourists, and consequently the itineraries that they plan and take. For researchers, there have been many exciting insights that have emerged from research that uses technology to understand mobility, along with a variety of learnings that challenge traditional theories regarding tourism movement. For example, repeat visitors, who were once argued as being focused on viewing big icons and covering large amounts of distance (McKercher et al., 2012) have also been found to be the most likely tourists to be found on discrete touring routes (Hardy et al., 2020).

The field of tourist tracking research is growing at a very rapid pace. A review in 2016 revealed that 45 journal articles existed in this space. As I collate this book, the number has at least doubled, and research in this space is growing at a rapid rate. In particular, the tracking of tourists using geo-tagged applications, GPS technology, mobile phone data and credit card data, now occupies a rapidly emerging and significant space within the field of tourism research.

Technology, disruptive innovations, big data, smart tourism and understanding mobility

The development of new technologies has also created an entirely new system of data collection, analysis and reporting. Schumpeter's (1934) seminal work on entrepreneurship and innovation defined innovations as new techniques or methods that enhance existing systems, but in the meantime cause the demise of existing systems. The work of Hall and Williams (2008) furthered Schumpeter's ideas and suggested that innovations can be evaluated in two ways – the form of the innovation, and the impact that the innovation has upon either industry sectors, regions, nations or the world.

Innovations are, according to Schumpeter's definition, inherently disruptive. The seminal work of Christensen (1997) defined disruptive innovation as new technologies that have different value propositions that give fringe and new customers something that they want. He suggested that while disruptive technologies may underperform in the shorter term, they may flourish in the long term and also cause larger companies to fail because of their disruption. In this book, many of the innovative techniques have done just that – they have forced tourism researchers to change the way they collect and analyse data.

Perhaps one of the most well-known disruptive innovations is the emergence of big data. Big data results from the collation of very large data sets that can be sourced from:

'…internet searches, credit card transactions, records of mobile phone activity, social networks, data on water and electricity consumption meteorological data, images recorded with video cameras' (Salas-Olmedo et al., 2018).

It is characterised as having three qualities (Salas-Olmedo et al., 2018):

1. Volume – as in terabytes or petabytes of data;
2. Velocity – data can be received in real time;
3. Variety – many sources can be used.

Big data has afforded researchers with the opportunity to collect vast amounts of data on mobility issues such as visitation flows, behaviour, infrastructure use, and the potential benefits mobility brings communities. Significantly, researchers can often access this data at low cost and in close to real time (Tenkanen et al., 2017). Consequently, big data offers a complement, if not a direct challenge, to surveys, which are unable to provide spatial and temporal behaviour in timely and accurate manner (Salas-Olmedo et al., 2018). Many readers will be aware of the Google Community Mobility reports that were generated during the COVID-19 pandemic by the digital traces of those using the Google app. These traces were collated and visualised in order to depict mobility and assist the tourism industry in understanding the impact of lockdown upon public transport and public park usage, plus retail, supermarket and the pharmacy sectors.

The uptake of technology and big data to inform decisions, along with the incorporation of technology into the tourism industry has led to the development of the concept of smart tourism, defined as:

'…tourism supported by integrated efforts at a destination to collect and aggregate/harness data derived from physical infrastructure, social connections, government/organizational sources and human bodies/ minds in combination with the use of advanced technologies to transform that data into on-site experiences and business value-propositions with a clear focus on efficiency, sustainability and experience enrichment.' (Gretzel et al., 2015: 181)

Arguably, understanding the range of options for collecting tourism data will assist destinations that wish to become smart tourism destinations.

Understanding mobility and spatiotemporal behaviour through technology: a brief review

The mobility paradigm places tourism at the core of social life, rather than the traditional view that tourism is an activity that is separate from daily life (Zheng et al., 2017; Coles and Hall, 2006; Franklin, 2003; den Hoed and Russo, 2017; Cohen et al., 2015). Technology has facilitated this change – prior to the introduction of technology and smart phones, travel was thought to be an activity that people took as a result of a perceived need to break away from work and responsibilities and recharge (e.g. Cohen, 1979; Krippendorff, 1987 and Graburn, 1983 took this perspective). Krippendorff (1987) argued that tourism was based on the premise of a separation from home and work life, and as such, the process of travel was seen as a transformative process that took place in distinct phases. Similarly, Clawson and Knetsch (1966) argued there were five phases of travel, beginning with anticipation and ending in reflection. The traditional phases of tourism planning, whereby one dreams, forms experiences and reflects, have become less prominent because of technology. Rather than needing to access information prior to their departure, tourists may now make plans en route, through their smartphones. Moreover, as a result of technology sharing (via travel blogs and social media), the reflection phase seems to have merged into the experiential/on-site phase, as photographs and status updates may be shared immediately. Technology has completely reconfigured the way we travel (Gretzel, 2011; Tussyadiah and Fesenmaier, 2009; Wang, Park and Fesenmaier, 2012). Consequently, the transformation from normal life to being a tourist arguably no longer involves distinct phases:

> 'The transformation that one underwent to become a tourist is no longer relevant as tourists remaining electronically linked to their home worlds as they explore their identity and the world of others' (Pearce, 2011: 41).

The new mobilities paradigm was coined by Hannam, Butler and Paris (2014) who argued that new technology is a key development in tourism mobility – it enables how we move, but also acts as a limitation.

The same authors also argue that the new mobilities paradigm has led to the development of new methodologies. They write:

'In any situation, mobilities involve the movement of people, the movement of a whole range of material things, and the movement of more intangible thoughts and fantasies. Mobilities also involve the use of a range of technologies both old and new. In short, proponents of the mobilities paradigm argue that the concept of mobilities is concerned with mapping and understanding both the large-scale movements of people, objects, capital and information across the world, as well as the more local processes of daily transportation, movement through public space, and the travel of material things within everyday life simultaneously.'
(Hannam, Butler and Paris, 2014: p. 172)

The mobilities paradigm places a focus on mapping and conceptualizing the movement of people and information around the globe. New technology is at the heart of this, and calls have been made for better theorization and research (Hannam, Sheller and Urry, 2006). Mobile phones are not only devices that connect tourists to their family and friends at home, they are also social objects that facilitate what has been described as a 'surveillance gaze' whereby they can create a virtual travel community that responds to each other's posts and watches each other travel (Hannam, Butler and Paris, 2014). As such, technology has enhanced the blurriness between everyday life and travel (Leurs and Hardy, 2018). This lack of separation and the continued use of technology whilst travelling means that vast amounts of data are being produced, allowing researchers to explore behaviour in unprecedented detail. Technology has allowed questions to be answered that surveys could not – for example, as the world has become increasingly globalized and borders in the EU have been removed, international tourism flows are often no longer recorded. Mobile phone data has offered an accurate, timely and detailed alternative to surveys and re-invigorated datasets on these flows of tourists (Ahas et al., 2008). Similarly accommodation statistics are very hard to collate, but big data sets such as mobile phone records, and data from location-enabled social media platforms such as Twitter, have proved to be reliable alternatives (Ahas et al., 2008).

Significantly, the uptake of new technologies has resulted in many conceptual insights into tourists' mobility and particularly that which is related to their behaviour in both time and space. Different forms of tracking methods have been applied to allow exploration of tourists' movement at multiple scales. These include tourists' movement within attractions, within destinations, between destinations and even between countries. Raun, Ahus and Tiru (2016) argued that new tracking technologies have afforded tourism destinations with five measurable dimensions that tourist movement can be measured against. These are spatial, temporal, compositional, social and dynamic dimensions.

Shoval (2012) argued that tourist tracking research has explored spatiotemporal movement in ways which can be categorised into seven themes. Arguably, since Shoval's seminal work, there are now two additional themes that tourist tracking researchers have tackled – automated modelling and the physiological effects of travel through time and space. Consequently, this book proposes that tourist tracking research tends to fit within at least one of the following themes:

1. **Descriptive analysis**: this form of research tends to explore the spatiotemporal aspects of tourists as case studies, with the objective of developing site specific insights. Recent examples of this include the research that was outlined by Hardy et al. (2020), who analysed tourists' behaviour in the island state of Tasmania, Australia.

2. **Development of predictive factors for spatiotemporal behaviour:** examples of research of this type includes that by Shoval et al. (2011), who developed predictions for the impacts that hotel location would have upon diurnal and spatial movement, and Raun, Shoval and Tiru's (2020) work that explored the impact that gateways have upon dispersal through destinations.

3. **Creation of typologies**: a body of research now exists where tourists have been segmented based on their spatiotemporal behaviour. Examples of this include work by Lewis and Hardy (2019) on wine tourists behaviour in southern Australia.

4. **Understanding tourists' decision–making choices:** tourist-tracking researchers have assessed the impact of motivation, socio-demographic factors, transport use, and previous travel behaviour on tourists' mobility and movement. Examples include McKercher et al. (2012), who assessed the impact of previous visitation on tourists' movement in a highly urbanised setting and found that first time visitors tend to focus on iconic attractions and 'sample' destinations, whereas repeat visitors tend to concentrate their visitation to certain activities. Other examples include the work of Hardy, Birenboim and Wells (2020), who compared the impact of different factors upon dispersal.

5. **Spatial correlation/abilities exploration:** this is where the research has focussed on how tourists orientate themselves and undertake wayfinding. An example of this is the work by Xia et al. (2008), who developed a measure that assessed the attractiveness of travel routes and tourist attractions, according to their spatial location and the time taken to move between attractions.

6. **Movement patterns and flow:** tourist tracking research of this nature seeks to determine patterns of movement within specific destinations. For example, the work of Yoshimura et al. (2014) used Bluetooth to track visitors' consumption of the Louvre in Paris, and research by Raun, Ahus and Tiru (2016) explored the relationship between home location and different travel patterns.

7. **Destination consumption:** big data from sources such as mobile phone data (Ahas et al., 2008) has proved particularly useful in identifying and managing congestion, along with research using data from Bluetooth and Wi-Fi that has been applied in both indoor and outdoor locations, including events and festivals (Versichele et al., 2014).

8. **Artificial intelligence and machine learning:** this form of tourist tracking research uses artificial intelligence and techniques such as machine learning or deep learning to develop predictions on how tourists will move through time and space (Hardy and Aryal, 2020).

9. **Physiological effects of tourist' mobility:** researchers are now combining techniques that assess emotional and physiological

1

responses to the spatiotemporal movement of tourists. Research by Kim and Fesenmaier (2015) explored the emotions of tourists using electro-dermal skin sensor technology. Following this, Shoval et al. (2018) explored tourists' physiological reactions to travel, and was able to determine where emotionally evocative areas existed for tourists as they moved through destinations.

Through the course of this book, the way in which different tracking techniques have contributed towards these nine categories will be explored in detail.

The ethics of tracking tourists

While information may be being produced constantly and in large volumes via technology, it is no longer considered ethical to assume that this data may be used freely. Only five years ago it was acceptable to collect user generated content – referred to as the democratisation of tourism information – as word of mouth sharing and feedback moved to online spaces and could be analysed and monitored automatically and in an extremely cost efficient manner. Many commercial business were developed to capitalise on this explosion of data, but the recent tightening of rules has rendered the use of big data, when no consent has been given, as non-ethical in many countries. This issue of ethics has risen to the forefront of many countries' media as the COVID-19 pandemic has taken hold and various contact-tracing apps have been developed to track citizens' movement and contacts, in order to attempt to slow the spread of the virus. Control of one's personal data is now a major societal issue. So what does this mean for research? How can research ethically collect tracking data? And what are the implication for participants who consent to tracking research? In Chapter 2, this book proposes a flexible ethical framework for researchers to consider when undertaking research. This framework may be utilised for all tracking studies, and is adjustable to ongoing legislative changes in this space.

Structure of the book

This book will examine different methodological approaches that may be undertaken to understand tourists' mobility. The structure is as follows:

Chapter 2 begins by reviewing what is meant by ethical approaches to tourist tracking research and changes in the way that the ethics of using tracking data have been viewed. The chapter focusses on legislation such as the European Union's General Data Protection Regulation (GDPR) and the impact that this has had upon the field of research. The chapter proposes a framework for the ethical conduct of tourist tracking research that is designed to ensure all facets of tourist tracking research are conducted with the highest possible standards.

Following this, Chapters 3 through to 10 review different tracking methods. The structure of each chapter is the same – they review how data is collected for each method, then the conceptual and methodological learnings that have emerged from the method are discussed. The chapters then review the advantages and limitations of each method, followed by their ethical implications. The following tourist tracking methods are reviewed:

- Chapter 3 - Survey research
- Chapter 4 - Global positioning systems
- Chapter 5 - Geo-tagged social media
- Chapter 6 - Continuous location-based data
- Chapter 7 - Mobile phone tower tracking
- Chapter 8 - Bluetooth and Wi-Fi
- Chapter 9 - Bespoke research apps
- Chapter 10 - Internet-based tracking

Chapter 11 is a review of emerging technologies, such as physiological tracking and artificial intelligence. The chapter concludes with a comparative synthesis of the different methods that can be used by future researchers wishing to select a tracking method that best suits their situation.

Key learnings from this chapter:

- Early methods of wayfinding and mobility have shaped the way we travel and record our movement.

- Technology sits at the heart of the new mobility paradigm.

- Technology has had profound impacts upon understanding tourists' movement and mobility.

- New technologies are changing the way in which we understand tourists' mobility and behaviour in both time and space.

- Ethical considerations should always underpin the decisions to engage with technology that tracks tourists' movement and mobility.

References

Ahas, R., Aasa, A., Roose, A., Mark, U. and Silm, S. (2008) Evaluating passive mobile positioning data for tourism surveys: An Estonian case study data, *Tourism Management*, 469-486.

Bates, E. S. (1911) *Touring in 1600: A Study in the Development of Travel as a Means of Education*, London: Constable.

Bukart, A. and Medlik, S. (1981) *Tourism: Past, Present and Future*, 2nd edition, London: Heinemann.

Baines, J. (2006) Travel in Third and Second Millennium Egypt, in C. Adams and J. Roy (eds), *Travel, Geography and Culture in Ancient Greece Egypt and the Near East*, Haverton: Oxbow Books, pp. 5-30.

Casson. L. (1974) *Travel in the Ancient World,* London: Allen and Unwin.

Christensen, C. (1997) *The Innovator's Dilemma: When new technologies cause great firms to fail*, Boston: Harvard Review Press.

Cioffi, R. (2016) Travel in the Roman World. *Oxford Handbooks Online,* 1–39, Available at: https://www.oxfordhandbooks.com/view/10.1093/oxfordhb/9780199935390.001.0001/oxfordhb-9780199935390-e-110 [Accessed 29 June 2020].

Clawson, M., and Knetsch,J. L. (1966) *Economics of Outdoor Recreation*, Baltimore, MD: John Hopkins University Press

Cohen, E. (1979) Rethinking the sociology of tourism, *Annals of Tourism Research*, **6**(1), 18-35.

Cohen, S.A., Duncan, T., Thulemark, M. (2015) Lifestyle mobilities: The crossroads of travel, leisure and migration, *Mobilities*, **10**, 155–172

Coles, T. and Hall, M. (2006) Editorial: The geography of tourism is dead. Long live geographies of tourism and mobility, *Current Issues in Tourism*, **9**, 289-292.

Coryat, T. (1611) *Coryat's Crudities*, (reprinted 1776), London: W. Cater. Available at: https://books.google.com.au/books?id=sGeowgOkNuIC [Accessed 12 August 2020].

Den Hoed, W. and Russo, A. P. (2017) Professional travellers and tourist practices, *Annals of Tourism Research*, **63**, 60–72.

Denny, M. (2012) *The Science of Navigation: From Dead Reckoning to GPS*, Baltimore: Johns Hopkins University Press.

Eccleston, R., Hardy, A. and Hyslop, S. (2020) Unlocking the potential of tracking technology for co-created tourism planning and development: Insights from the Tourism Tracer Tasmania project, *Tourism Planning & Development*, **17**(1) 82-95.

Feifer, M. (1985) *Going Places: Tourism in history*, New York: Stein and Day.

Franklin, A. (2003) *Tourism: An introduction,* London: Sage.

Graburn, N. H. (1983) The anthropology of tourism, *Annals of Tourism Research*, **10**(1), 9-33.

Gretzel, U. (2011) Intelligent systems in tourism: A social science perspective, *Annals of Tourism*, **38** (3), 757–779.

Gretzel, U., Sigala, M., Xiang, Z. and Koo, C. (2015) Smart tourism: foundations and developments, *Electronic Markets*, **25**(3), 179-188.

Hall, C.M. and Williams, A.M. (2008) *Tourism and Innovation,* London: Routledge.

Hannam, K., Butler, G., and Paris, C. M. (2014) Developments and key issues in tourism mobilities, *Annals of Tourism Research*, **44**, 171-185.

Hannam, K., Sheller, M. and Urry, J. (2006) Editorial: mobilities, immobilities and mooring, *Mobilities,* **1**(1), 1-22.

Hardy, A., and Aryal, J. (2020) Using innovations to understand tourist mobility in national parks, *Journal of Sustainable Tourism*, **28**(2), 263-283.

Hardy, A. and Birenboim, A. and Wells, M. (2020), Using geoinformatics to assess tourist dispersal at the state level, *Annals of Tourism Research*, **82**,102903.

Hardy, A., Eccleston, R.G., Tinch, D., Hyslop, S., Booth, K., Robards, B., Wong, T.L and Aryal, J., (2020) Innovations in research technology: the case of tourism tracer, in C.S. Ooi & A. Hardy (Eds), *Tourism in Tasmania*, Hobart, Tasmania: Forty South Publishing, 175-185.

Hern, A. (1967) *The Seaside Holiday: The history of the English seaside resort*, London: Cresset Press.

Herodotus (1921) *Herodotus: The Histories*, Digital version in Perseus Digital Library online: A.D. Godley (ed.), London; New York: Loeb Classical Library

Hirth, F. (1906) Origin of the mariner's compass in China, *The Monist*, **16** (3), 321-330.

Kim, J. J. and Fesenmaier, D. R. (2015) Measuring emotions in real time: implications for tourism experience design, *Journal of Travel Research*, **54**(4), 419–29.

Krippendorff, J. (1987) *The Holiday Makers: Understanding the impacts of leisure and travel*, London: Heinemann.

Lane, F. (1963) The economic meaning of the invention of the compass, *The American Historical Review*, **68** (3), 605-617.

Lewis, G. and Hardy, A. (2019) Wine tourists in Tasmania: An exploratory project using tourism tracer data, Unpublished report prepared by the University of Tasmania for Wine Tasmania. Hobart, Tasmania: University of Tasmania.

Leurs, E. and Hardy, A. (2018) Tinder tourism: Tourist experiences beyond the tourism industry realm, *Annals of Leisure Research* **22** (3), 323-341.

McKercher, B., Shoval, N., Ng, E. and Birenboim, A. (2012) First and repeat visitor behaviour: GPS tracking and GIS analysis in Hong Kong, *Tourism Geographies*, **14**(1), 147-161

Mead, W. E. (1914) *The Grand Tour in the Eighteenth Century*, New York: Houghton Mifflin

Parks, G.B. (1954) *The English Traveler to Italy*, Rome: Edizioni di storia e letteratura.

Pearce, P. L. (2011) *Tourist Behaviour and the Contemporary World*, Vol. 51, Channel View Publications.

Pimlott, J. (1947) *The Englishman's Holiday: A Social History*, London: Faber & Faber.

Raun, J., Shoval, N. and Tiru, M. (2020) Gateways for intra-national tourism flows: measured using two types of tracking technologies, *International Journal of Tourism Cities*, **6** (2), 261-278.

Raun, J. Ahas, R. and Tiru, M. (2016) Measuring tourism destinations using mobile tracking data, *Tourism Management* **57**, 202-212.

Richardson, J. (1722) *An Account of Some of the Statues, Bas-Reliefs, Drawings, and Pictures in Italy*, The Crown, St Pauls Church Yard, London.

Robinson, H. (1976) *A Geography of Tourism*, Harlow: Longman.

Salas-Olmedo, M.H., Moya-Gómez, B., García-Palomares, J.C. and Gutiérrez, J. (2018) Tourists' digital footprint in cities: Comparing Big Data sources, *Tourism Management,* **66**, 13-25.

Schumpeter, J. (1934) *The Theory of Economic Development,* Cambridge: Harvard University Press.

Schwab, K. (2016) *The Fourth Industrial Revolution.* Geneva: World Economic Forum.

Sen, T. (2001) The travel records of Chinese pilgrims Faxian, Xuanzang, and Yijing: Sources for cross-cultural encounters between Ancient China and Ancient India, *Education about Asia,* **11** (3), 24- 33.

Shoval, N. (2012). Time geography and tourism, In *The Routledge Handbook of Tourism Geographies* (189-195), Routledge.

Shoval, N., McKercher, B., Ng, E. and Birenboim, A. (2011) Hotel location and tourism activity in cities. *Annals of Tourism Research,* **38**(4): 1594-1612.

Shoval, N., Schvimer, Y. and Tamir, M., (2018) Real-time measurement of tourists' objective and subjective emotions in time and space, *Journal of Travel Research,* **57**(1) 3–16.

Tenkanen, T., Di Minin, E. Heikinheimo, V., Hausmann, A., Her, M., Kajala, L. and Toivonen. T. (2017) Instagram, Flickr, or Twitter: Assessing the usability of social media data for visitor monitoring in protected areas, *Scientific Reports,* **7**(1), 1-11.

Tussyadiah, I. (2020) A review of research into automation in tourism: Launching the Annals of Tourism Research curated collection on artificial intelligence and robotics in tourism, *Annals of Tourism Research,* **81**.

Tussyadiah, I. and Fesenmaier, D. (2009) Mediating tourist experiences: Access to places via shared videos, *Annals of Tourism Research,* **36**(1), 24–40.

Versichele, M., Neutens, T., Claeys Bouuaert, M. and Van de Weghe, N. (2014) Time-geographic derivation of feasible co-presence opportunities from network-constrained episodic movement data, *Transactions in GIS,* **18**(5), 687-703.

Wang, D., Park, S. and Fesenmaier, D. (2012) The role of smartphones in mediating the touristic experience, *Journal of Travel Research,* **51**(4), 371–387.

Xia, J. C., Arrowsmith, C., Jackson, M. and Cartwright, W. (2008) The wayfinding process relationships between decision-making and landmark utility, *Tourism Management,* **29**(3), 445-457.

Yang, E., Khoo-Lattimore, C. and Arcodia, C. (2017) A narrative review of Asian female travellers: looking into the future through the past, *Current Issues in Tourism,* **20**(10), 1008-1027.

Yoshimura, Y., Sobolevsky, S., Ratti, C., Girardin, F., Carrascal, J. P., Blat, J. and Sinatra, R. (2014) An analysis of visitors' behavior in the Louvre Museum: A study using Bluetooth data, *Environment and Planning B: Planning and Design,* **41**(6), 1113-1131.

Zarocostas, J. (2020), How to fight an infodemic, *The Lancet,* **395**, 676.

Zheng, W., Huang, X., and Li, Y. (2017) Understanding the tourist mobility using GPS: Where is the next place?, *Tourism Management,* **59**, 267-280.

2 The Ethics of Tracking

What this chapter will cover:

- Rising concerns over tracking and breaches of privacy.

- Steps that should be taken in order to ensure an ethical tracking approach to research.

- The importance of considering socio-cultural attitudes towards tracking.

- The importance of abiding by legislation, platform terms and conditions, and gaining participants' consent, where possible.

- An ethical framework that should be followed by researchers who wish to engage in tourist tracking research.

Introduction

Research that tracks tourists' movement challenges our perception of ethics, privacy, and consent. The introduction of technology with the capability to track tourists in fine grained detail is viewed by some as a gross invasion of privacy, by others as a personal safety mechanism, and is treated by others with almost complete ambivalence. Importantly, in the past fifteen years we have witnessed a great change in the way in which tracking has been viewed by study participants and the general public, along with many mysterious contradictions in our acceptance or resistance to privacy – possibly fueled by media attention around this issue.

In the early 2000s, apps began emerging that conducted GPS tracking covertly in the background. For example, flash light applications (henceforth referred to as 'apps') that many of us had on our mobile phones, appeared to be a useful app. However, the business model of these apps was that they tracked users' movements in the background of the app and on-sold this data to marketing companies. Similarly, The Weather Channel app was recently exposed for on-selling tracking data that was covertly collected, resulting in a legal case against its owner, IBM. In 2017, it was estimated that 70% of apps track and share user information with third parties (Vallina-Roderigue and Sundaresan, 2017).

While there is resistance to some forms of tracking, there appears to be acceptance of other types. Strava is one such example. It is estimated that each week, 8 million activities are uploaded onto the app (Goode, 2017). Every 40 days, the app adds one million users (Craft, 2018). It is used by recreational hikers, bikers and runners, who wish to track and share their activities. It is widely known that the business model of Strava is built upon on-selling this data to cities and councils. This practice seems to be widely accepted by users.

Conversely, recent research illustrated that 23.1% of adults in the USA have enabled the Do Not Track settings on their internet browsers. This is a voluntary signal that is not required to be respected by tech companies. Google, Facebook and Twitter, for example, allegedly do not respect this request (DuckDuckGo, 2019). The Cambridge Analytica scandal in early 2018 clearly illustrated these concerns. The British political consulting firm was exposed as unlawfully using Facebook data and manipulating political messages in order to affect political campaigns. The scandal highlighted the use of apps to collate user data and resulted in great losses in credibility to the Facebook brand.

What becomes apparent in reactions to news of digital tracking is that individuals vary widely in their belief systems regarding tracking. It is therefore critical that researchers who wish to engage in tracking research must engage in ethical research practices. This it not only an ethical issue but also a legal one; many countries now have legislation pertaining to the collation, use and dissemination of personal data.

The development of an ethical tracking framework

The model that is proposed below is an extension of previous work by Hardy et al. (2017), who proposed an approach to designing ethical tourist tracking research. This model places emphasis on the creation of an ethical framework, whereby tourist tracking research design is driven by, rather than reacts to, ethical approaches to research. In particular, the model considers regions' socio-cultural contexts, the legislative environment, recruitment of participants (if required), and the terms and conditions of data, should user generated content be the primary data source. This model is built upon a framework for social media research that was developed by Townsend and Wallace (2016) — explored in detail in Chapter 5. The elements of this ethical approach to tourist tracking research model will now be discussed.

2

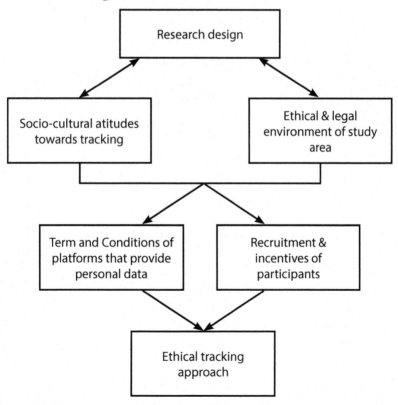

Figure 2.1: A model for developing an ethical tracking framework

1. Research design

Research design methods should be designed so that they simultaneously seek to answer research questions in an ethical and legally appropriate manner. The following aspects need to be considered:

2a. Socio-cultural attitudes towards tracking

Recent research by Hardy and Wells (2019) identified cultural differences in willingness to take part in tracking research. This concurred with previous research that determined scepticism towards tracking research by some segments of international tourists and the need to consider cultural factors that may influence the perceived credibility of research projects (Hardy et al., 2017). Therefore, it is important that researchers gauge social attitudes towards tracking amongst both residents of their study area and visitors to it, to ensure their methods are deemed acceptable. These attitudes can change very rapidly – breaches of privacy by large companies have often resulted in much angst over tracking, while the COVID-19 pandemic has highlighted the benefits of tracking via apps such as Singapore's Trace Together app, which has, in some jurisdictions, enhanced the reputation of ethical tracking. Thus, while a research design may be elected that is entirely suited to the research question, if the methods selected are not socially acceptable in the study region at the time of the study, then this model argues that such an approach could not be considered to be ethical. Thus, a feedback loop exists between the first step of research design and socio-cultural attitudes.

2b. Ethical/legal environment of the study region

Researchers must ensure that their research complies with the requirements of the research institute in which their research is undertaken, along with the legal requirements of their state and/or country. For researchers who wish to recruit participants to track tourists' mobility, there are national guidelines that must be abided by. In Australia, a *National Statement on the Ethical Conduct of Research (2007)* (Australian Government and Universities Australia, 2018) has been developed for anyone undertaking research with human participants. It states that if researchers wish to recruit participants (this is relevant for the approaches outlined in Chapters 3, 4, 6 and 9), they must clearly undertake the following actions: state the research purpose and methods, not coerce participants into participation, allow participants to opt-in freely, and allow individuals to withdraw themselves and their data from the study without consequence. As a result of national guidelines such as these, many research institutions have developed ethics committees and researchers must have their research plans approved via these committees, prior to its commencement.

For researchers who wish to use personal data such as user-generated content, Kozinets (2019) argues that the European Union's (2016) General Data Protection Regulation (GDPR) is regarded as the default international standard for the use of personal data, such as that which is generated through technology, online activities and mobile phone data. The GDPR is particularly relevant for techniques outlined in Chapters 5, 7, 8 and 10. The GDPR applies to companies or organisations that are based in the European Union that use personal data as part of their business. It also applies to researchers outside of the EU who monitor the behaviour of EU residents or offer goods or services to residents of the EU.

The GDPR states that the default position should be that individuals be given the opportunity to opt-in and have their data used, rather than opt-out. It also sets out rules that institutions must abide by in relation to the collection, use, disclosure, storage, and handling of personal data. Significantly, research is said to occupy a privileged position within the GDPR. Kozinets (2019: 225) writes that:

> '...the GDPR permits the collection of public data for research purposes by legitimate research actors who are processing data for purposes that are in the public interest, including scientific and historical research purposes, as long as the researcher (or 'data controller') acts in keeping with the recognized standards for scientific research.'

Such is the impact of the GDPR that it has triggered legislative changes regarding data privacy in many other countries.

Finally, it is important to note that ethical research conduct and legislation pertaining to data privacy is a rapidly changing landscape. Researchers need to keep abreast of these changes and review the legal rules of their country and region before embarking on research of this nature. As with step 2a, if the methods selected are not ethically/legally appropriate for the study region, then this model argues that such an approach should not be considered to ethical. Thus, a feedback loop exists between the first step of research design and 2b.

3a. Terms and Conditions of platforms that provide personal data

For researchers who wish to use personal data, the Terms and Conditions of the platforms from which they wish to collate the data must also be considered, in order to ensure ethical collation of the data. As is discussed in detail in Chapter 5, in the context of social media platforms, many apps now stipulate the means by which data is collected. There is now an almost ubiquitous use of automated scraping techniques, such as employing bots written in Python. Some platforms such as Twitter provide automated data sets via an Application Programming Interface (API) which is a software conduit that allows two different applications to communicate and share data with each other. Other apps, such as Instagram, forbid scraping and do not provide APIs, thus the only option for researchers is to manually collate data. For researchers using mobile phone data or other user generated data, such as ticketing purchases, it is also important that the Terms and Conditions of the data carriers are abided by, as well as the conditions that individuals agreed to when using the mobile phone or ticketing company.

3b. Recruitment and incentives of participants

Some forms of tracking – outlined in Chapters 3, 4, 6 and 9 – require recruitment of participants. As mentioned, the guiding principles of informed consent is that data privacy and protection must underpin research of this type. Ethical research practice should also consider the burden that research of this nature may place upon participants, including the requirement to fill out paperwork and wear, carry or engage with devices and/or apps. It is at this stage that the attractiveness of the research approach to the participants, who are travelling in their leisure or business time, becomes significant and should be kept in mind.

Conclusion

Researchers who wish to undertake research that explores tourist behaviour through time and space must, like all researchers, follow ethical research conduct. However, tracking differs from more traditional forms of research because in recent years it is has been the subject of much media attention, much of it negative, as it has exposed the unlawful use of data. As a consequence, research of this type could be regarded as having 'emotional baggage'. It is essential that researchers are sensitive to the perception regarding tracking within the community that that they are studying, as well as amongst tourists that they are researching. This consideration must be made alongside the legislative and ethical conventions for their research area. Provided this is done, ethical research conduct will prevail.

Key learnings from this chapter:

- There are divisions and contention that surround the issue of tracking, often with regards to the issues of informed consent.

- Ethical considerations should always underpin the decisions to engage with technology that tracks tourists' movement and mobility.

- Researchers must consider multiple issues when undertaking tourist tracking research.

- An ethical tracking framework can assist researchers to take reasonable steps to ensure their research abides by their regions, institutions and technological platforms' ethical and privacy regulations.

References

Craft, S. (2018) With time at Instagram and Facebook to leverage, Strava CEO James Quarles wants to make his fitness tracking app a community for the most engaged athletes in the world, *In The Black,* 01 May, Available at: https://www.intheblack.com/articles/2018/05/01/james-quarles-strava [Accessed 13 August, 2020]

DuckDuckGo (2019) The "Do Not Track" setting doesn't stop you from being tracked, *DuckDuckGo Blog,* 5 February, Available at: https://spreadprivacy.com/do-not-track/ [Accessed 13 August, 2020]

European Union (2016) *General Data Protection Regulation* (GDPR), Available at: https://gdpr-info.eu/ [Accessed 21 July, 2020].

Goode, L. (2017) Fitness app Strava really, really wants to be the social network for athletes, *The Verge,* May 2, 2017, Available at: https://www.theverge.com/2017/5/2/15511118/strava-fitness-tracking-app-athlete-posts-social-network [Accessed 13 August, 2020].

Hardy, A. and Wells, M. (2019) *Recruiting Tracking Participants in Skåne, Sweden.* Unpublished report for Tourism Skåne.

Hardy, A., Hyslop, S., Booth, K., Robards, B., Aryal, J., Gretzel, U. and Eccleston, R. (2017) Tracking tourists' travel with smartphone-based GPS technology: a methodological discussion, *Journal of Information Technology & Tourism,* **17**(3), 255-274.

Kozinets, R. (2019) *Netnography: The Essential Guide to Qualitative Social Media Research.* Third Edition, SAGE Publications.

Australian Government and Universities Australia. (2018) *National Statement on Ethical Conduct in Human Research 2007 (updated 2018).* Australian Government, Canberra. Available from https://www.nhmrc.gov.au/about-us/publications/national-statement-ethical-conduct-human-research-2007-updated-2018 [Accessed 27th August 2019].

Townsend, L. and Wallace, C. (2016) Social media research: A guide to ethics, University of Aberdeen working paper, Available at: https://www.gla.ac.uk/media/Media_487729_smxx.pdf. [Accessed 4 February, 2020].

Vallina-Roderiguez, N. and Sundaresan, S. (2017) 7 in 10 smartphone apps share your data with third-party services, *The Conversation,* May 30, Available at: http://theconversation.com/7-in-10-smartphone-apps-share-your-data-with-third-party-services-72404 [Accessed 6th July, 2020].

3 Understanding Tourists' Movement via Survey Research

What this chapter will cover:

- The role that surveys have played in understanding tourists' behaviour and movement within and between countries.

- The significance of survey research, given its ability to collect socio-demographic and traveller behaviour data.

- The challenges that survey research poses to tourist tracking researchers, given its inability to collect accurate spatio-temporal data.

- The considerations that researchers must take to use survey research in an ethical manner.

Introduction

One of the most significant gaps in tourism research is also one of the simplest questions to ask: Where do different types of tourists go? Surveys have played a very important role in this space. They have been used to determine the characteristics of travellers such as their behavioural preferences, their expenditure and the destinations that tourists have travelled to. Prior to the technological era, surveys were one of the few means by which tourists' movement could be tracked. However, the advent of technology has exposed the weaknesses of survey research. While surveys perform a very important role in understanding some aspects of mobility, they must be viewed with caution. This chapter will explore the strengths, weaknesses and conceptual outcomes that have emerged from this method of tracking.

What surveys tell us about tourists' movement

There are a variety of early studies that used survey data to understand tourist flows between countries. These have played a major role in assisting in understanding how tourists move within destinations and between destinations, such as in relation to international tourist flows.

International tourist movement

Early examples of international tourist flow studies include Williams and Zelinsky (1970), who assessed international tourist flows using data from the International Union of Official Travel Organizations. The authors noted that the survey data, while useful, was subject to challenges. These included double counting when the same tourists crossed multiple European borders, missing data from countries who did not collect survey data, and the lack of corresponding demographic data. However, they noted that despite the limitations with international survey data sets, there were countries whose international flow data was consistent and more robust than others. The authors developed a predictive model based upon the flow assignment model developed by Goodman (Goodman, 1963, and 1964) and argued that flows are patterned and not random.

There have been many examples of survey research that has resulted in further conceptual advances in our understanding how international tourists move through destinations. McKercher and Lew (2003) used survey research to explore the concept of Distance Decay. They conducted telephone surveys of Hong Kong residents who had undertaken an international pleasure trip, and concluded that distance has a decaying effect on demand for international travel – demand for tourism reliant on airlines decreases with distance. The authors defined Effective Tourism Exclusion Zones (ETEZ) as regions where little or no tourism occurs due to distance from a source market. ETEZs create demand curves that have very low demand very close to the source, followed by a peak in demand at a short distance from to the source, followed by a rapid decrease in demand as distance increases (see Figure 3.1). McKercher and Lew's (2003) research found that shorter distance trips tend to be characteristic of trips taken in the spatial area that is located before the ETEZs. Conversely, trips taken beyond the ETEZ zone tend to be longer in duration, involve multiple stops and have a strong touring element.

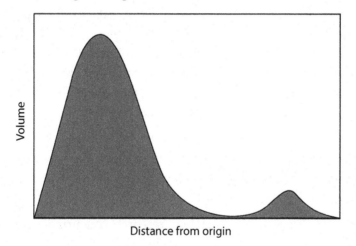

Figure 3.1: McKercher and Lew's Effective Tourism Exclusion Zones demand curve, including a secondary peak. Adapted from McKercher and Lew, (2003).

Intranational and intra-destination movement

Survey research has also resulted in conceptual understandings of how tourists move through countries and destinations. Early survey research by Forer and Pearce (1984) mapped the itineraries of package tourists in New Zealand. There is also a small body of work mapping independent travellers; Mings and McHugh (1992) used survey data to develop a proposition that at the intra-destination level, two characteristics affect movement of independent travellers: destination characteristics and tourist characteristics. They proposed four trip configurations: the direct route; partial orbit; full orbit and fly drive patterns.

Oppermann's (1992) survey research assessed intranational tourist flows via a survey of 1000 departing visitors in Malaysia. The survey asked tourists to detail their spatial behaviour in Malaysia, including where and how long they stayed overnight, their entry and departure points, and their travel routes. This resulted in an understanding of flows and highlighted areas of concentration, directionality, and market segment dispersion.

In further research using this same dataset, Oppermann (1995) proposed seven possible itinerary types, including two single and five multi-destination itineraries. Flogenfeldt (1999) also defined several itineraries within Norway, including the day trip, the resort trip, the base holiday trip and the round trip. The author argued that nationality alone does not influence the itinerary that visitors take. More recently at a country level, the work of Becken et al. (2007) used survey data from the New Zealand International Visitor Survey and the New Zealand Domestic Travel Study to describe passenger movements and develop visitor flow models for the country.

Within Australia, Tideswell and Faulkner (1999) used the Queensland Visitor Survey data to assess tourists' propensity to visit multiple destinations in regional areas. The authors assessed a number of factors, including:

1. **Purpose of visit**: their research concurred with Oppermann's (1992) earlier work and found that visitors nominating pleasure/ holiday as the main purpose of travel are more likely to visit multiple destinations.

2. **Travel party size**: their findings also concurred with Opermann's suggestion that multi-destination itineraries are more likely to be taken by small travel parties.

3. **Long haul visitors:** their research concluded that long haul visitors are more likely to visit multiple destinations.

4. **Transport**: the study supported work by Debbage (1991) and argued that those in rental or private vehicles are more likely to visit multiple destinations.

5. **Information sources**: the study concluded that those who use just one source of information on Queensland prior to their arrival were less likely to undertake multi-destination travel.

At the intra-destination scale, Lau and McKercher's (2004) study of first and repeat visitors explored, via a survey, the movement of visitors to Hong Kong. As well as determining that first and repeat visitors have different motives, the study illustrated that first-time visitors tend to travel widely through regions in order to visit iconic attractions. Conversely, they found that repeat visitors are more likely to shop and dine. Freytag (2010) concurred with this finding through survey research, suggesting that repeat visitors are not as homogeneous, stay off the beaten track, try harder to participate in the daily life of locals and follow specific interests that relate to the destination – such as learning the language or staying longer at points of interest.

In further research, the same authors (McKercher and Lau, 2008) used survey and GIS mapping to assess tourists' movement within destinations. They developed 11 trip styles built upon the conceptual propositions made by Lew and McKercher (2006) who proposed seven types of movement patterns. McKercher and Lau (2008) argued that intra-destination movement is influenced by two factors: territoriality and linearity. Territoriality refers to the distance travelled from the hotel, and linearity refers to the movement patterns that are created by the tourists. While McKercher and Lau (2008) supported the territory dimension, the 'path' argument was questioned. Rather it was found that the number of stops made during the day (intensity) and whether tourists confine their movements to a specific node or wander through a destination (specificity) influence spatial patterns (McKercher and Lau 2008) (see Figure 3.2). They identified 11 trip styles:

1. No movement beyond the hotel;
2. Unspecified local exploration within 500m of accommodation;
3. Local exploration with specified stops;
4. Single distant stop – travel more than 500m from accommodation to an attraction or attraction node;
5. Multiple distant stops – travel more than 500m from accommodation to multiple attractions or attraction nodes;
6. Local exploration and a single distant stop – travel within 500m of the accommodation plus travel more than 500m from the hotel to an attraction or attraction node;

7. Local exploration and multiple distant stops – travel within 500m of accommodation and travel more than 500m to more than one attraction or attraction nodes;

8. Multiple trips in one day, with returns to accommodation between trips;

9. Inter-destination travel – day trip to a nearby destination;

10. Tour with or without other activity – commercial sightseeing tour;

11. Multiple day trips including a tour as one of the trips.

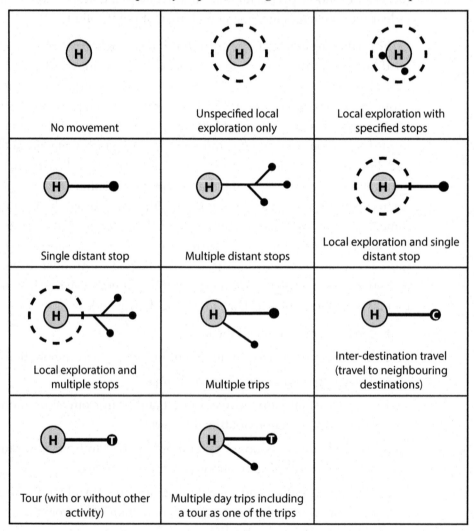

Figure 3.2: McKercher and Lau's eleven trip styles. Adapted from McKercher and Lau (2008).

Survey research has also resulted in the development of theories on the factors that influence tourists' movement patterns within destinations. Lau and McKercher (2006) argued that three sets of factors influence tourists' movement. The first of these are human factors such as tourist route, travel party, personal motivations, previous visits. Human factors have been studied in detail and identified by a variety of authors: Freytag, (2010); McKercher et al. (2012), and McKercher and Zoltan (2014). The second set of factors that influence intra-destination movement are physical factors such as destination geomorphology, weather and configuration of the destination in terms of transport corridors and location of attractions (Lau and McKercher, 2006). Connell and Page (2008) argued that gateways and egress points were important in influencing movement patterns; their study found a hierarchy of gateways when studying movements through a national park region. In further work, Becken and Wilson (2013) administered surveys to international tourists at the end of their trips to New Zealand to determine how weather affects travel. They found that most tourists (63%) made some changes to their trip while travelling due to weather. The third factor that Lau and McKercher's (2006) survey research demonstrated as being important was time – both length of stay in a destination and total trip duration.

More recently, Masiero and Zoltan (2013) used survey research to assess transport choice and how it impacts intra-destination movement. They argued that tourists' decision over how much area they will cover is inevitably linked to their choice of transport – especially public vs private transport. They argued that movement patterns are not affected by demographic variables, but trip characteristics play an important role in determining them. This was demonstrated by the high positive impact of repeat visits and commercial attractions – thus confirming Lew and McKercher's (2006) conceptual theory that trip behavioural variables (such as familiarity with the destination) are the most influential determinants of destination movement patterns and can be used to predict the extent of that area that is visited.

In addition to being used to understand the factors that influence intra-destination movement, survey research has also been used to quantify and measure movement. Researchers such as Lau et al. (2017) have used survey data to develop indices, such as the Gini index, to determine seasonal fluctuations in tourism dispersal and the spatial distribution of international tourists in Australia. Survey data has been described as an effective means to measure dispersal. In the island state of Tasmania, the government stance is that dispersal is regarded as occurring when a tourist spends at least one night outside the geographical boundaries of its two largest cities, Hobart and Launceston. Ratios such as these do not require high spatial resolution. (Hardy, Birenboim and Wells, 2020). While survey data is not adequate for inferring the spatial magnitude of dispersal, dispersal ratios that are derived from surveys are useful tools for understanding the magnitude of tourism in terms of both numbers and expenditure in core and regional areas (Hardy, Birenboim and Wells, 2020).

Significantly, while survey research has resulted in many theoretical conceptualisations of tourists' movement, it has been noted that survey research "cannot capture the actual path of each tourist" (Lew and McKercher (2006). Despite this limitation, travel pattern or itinerary mapping via surveys has proved useful because it has illustrated which vehicle routes are used in specific areas; it has allowed analysis of tourist flows to be undertaken; has illustrated where tourists stop; and highlighted what activities they undertake on different routes. This provides an important compliment to traditional surveys that have tended to focus on the demographic or psychographic characteristics of tourists (Connell and Page, 2008). However, Shoval, McKercher, Ng and Birenboim (2011) note the complexities of mapping – at first glance it seems to be simple to map itineraries, but it becomes extremely complicated because individuals' movements vary so much. Rather than developing itineraries, Huang and Wu (2012) conducted a survey of tourists to the Summer Palace in Beijing and offered an alternative typology. They concluded that four dimensions should be used to describe tourist behavioural patterns: temporal factors, spatial behavioural factors, activity choice factors, and path factors. The authors found that when studying their single attraction, temporal behaviour factors played the most important role in clustering, and specifically entry and exit times made the largest contribution to the cluster analysis. Moreover, they found that when time was short, tourists' use of space was conserved, furthermore when travel time decreased, so too did stay time.

Advantages of survey research

Survey research requires the development of a paper or online tool that is relatively cheap to implement. There is no requirement for apps to be developed, programs or code to be written to scrape data, or for GPS loggers to be purchased. Surveys are particularly useful for understanding the characteristics of tourists arriving at destinations, including their demographic characteristics, their past travel behaviour, and their attitudes towards travel. Surveys are also useful for understanding expenditure, although the accuracy of the results should be viewed with caution; the reasons for this are discussed below under challenges.

In terms of travel behaviour, when recruitment is designed to represent populations, surveys can be very useful in understanding the percentages and characteristics of tourists who visit destinations or attractions. Data on movement within destinations and attractions can also be gained using maps placed within surveys that allow tourists to indicate where and when they have travelled. This data should be viewed with caution however, as it is time-consuming to analyse, is subject to the ability of the respondent to recollect their spatial and temporal movements, and the data is coarse.

That said, fine grained, highly precise movement data is not always required. If researchers require information that determines how far tourists have travelled (linear distance), survey research has also been posited as appropriate (Hardy, Birenboim and Wells, 2020). Linear distance can be calculated by measuring the maximum distance between the two most distant GPS points for each participant. Cumulative distance may also be calculated from hand drawn maps, which is the total mileage a tourists has travelled. It has been suggested that it is appropriate to collect both these forms of data through surveys (Hardy, Birenboim and Wells, 2020).

Challenges of survey research

The limitations of survey research have been well documented in literature that extends beyond tracking research. The length of surveys can be regarded as tedious to tourists, who are highly mobile people, and who are often using their leisure time (Dolnicar and Grün, 2013). Surveys have also been documented as being prone to asking questions that are problematic. For example, scales that ask participants to rank issues and experiences from 1 to 7 have been demonstrated as being particularly unstable as participants often tend to tick the same number repetitively, due to the time they take to read and complete (Dolnicar and Grün, 2013). There are also vast differences in how respondents complete surveys. Recent eye-tracking research demonstrated that how respondents view surveys differs greatly, which impacts the way in which survey questions are answered (Brosnan et al., 2019). Furthermore, it must be remembered that surveys assume literacy. A study found functional adult literacy in Tasmania, Australia to be only 49%, making it the lowest adult literacy in all states of Australia (Australian Bureau of Statistics, 2013). This meant that half of adult Tasmanians lack the literacy skills necessary to cope with the demands of everyday life and work, and thus would be incapable of undertaking a self-completed questionnaire (Hardy and Pearson, 2016). These challenges are compounded by the fact that significant differences exist in how participants from different cultures respond to surveys; this was noted as a limitation of the survey method by Dolnicar and Grün (2007).

When trying to use surveys to decipher movement, several challenges have also been noted. Surveys are often done at the end of travellers' journeys, asking them to recall how much money they have spent and where they have been. This process of recollection is not always accurate and is reliant on how well survey participants are able to recollect their movements through unfamiliar locations (Shoval and Isaacson, 2007; McKercher and Zoltan, 2014). Moreover, tracking research requires precision in terms of tourists' movement. Surveys may include a list that tourists select from to record their movement, or, in some cases, a map where tourists are asked to mark their movement and/or directionality. This produces coarse data which may be useful in some instances but is not detailed enough for nuanced understandings of tourists' movement.

Ethical implications for survey research

The creation of a survey requires question design and recruitment of participants to answer the questions. There is agreement that ethical survey practice should involve: the development of questions that seek to answer the research question, transparency of the research project and process, disclosure of the methods and procedures that seek to accurately address the research questions, and assurances of confidentiality and/ or anonymity to participants (Oldendick, 2012). As surveys require participation, researchers should also consider who is being recruited in order to avoid bias, and they must also ensure that coercion for involvement does not occur during recruitment, or when the survey questions are being answered by the participant.

Researchers must also abide by the ethical requirements of their county and institution, as outlined in Chapter 2. For example, in Australia the *National Statement on Ethical Conduct in Human Research* (Commonwealth of Australia, 2018) states that participants must be made aware of what the study involves, should be invited to opt-in rather than opt out, should be able to withdraw themselves and their data from the study at any time; must be made aware of the risks, if any, of being involved; and must be given the opportunity to be given feedback on the results of the study (Commonwealth of Australia, 2018).

Conclusion

Survey research has resulted in a variety of conceptual advances in understanding how tourists travel between international countries, how they travel within countries and also how they travel within destinations and attractions. They are particularly useful for understanding the demographic characteristics of tourists moving through locations and their attitudes towards travel. They are also cheap and relatively easy to design and implement as little technology is required. However, surveys have a variety of limitations. Recall, responder bias and literacy are perhaps the most problematic of these, as they can compromise the ability to collate accurate insights into tourists' movement. Researchers who choose to use this method are well advised to bear these issues in mind when selecting this method, which performs far better over the short term, when recollection of the fine details of travel is not required to be documented.

Key learnings from this chapter:

- Survey data has resulted in considerable insights into tourists' international and intra-country movement.

- Survey methods can provide useful data on tourists' socio-demographic status and past travel behaviour.

- Survey research is limited in its ability to provide fine grained, detailed spatio- temporal data, as recall is a major issue for participants.

- The non-covert manner of survey research means that informed consent can be gained from participants.

References

Australian Bureau of Statistics, (2013) *Adult Literacy and Life Skills Survey 2011-2012*. Canberra, Australia.

Becken, S. and Wilson, J. (2013) The impacts of weather on tourist travel, *Tourism Geographies*, **15**(4), 620-639.

Becken, S., Vuletich, S. and Campbell, S. (2007) Developing a GIS-supported tourist flow model for New Zealand, pp. 107-122 in D. Airey, J. Tribe (Eds.), *Progress in Tourism Research*, Elsevier, Oxford.

Brosnan, K., Babakhani, N. and Dolnicar, S. (2019) 'I know what you're gonna ask me' - Why respondents don't read survey questions, *International Journal of Market Research*, **61**(1), 366-379.

Commonwealth of Australia (2018) *National Statement on Ethical Conduct in Human Research*. The National Health and Medical Research Council, the Australian Research Council and Universities Australia.

Connell, J. and Page, S. (2008) Exploring the spatial patterns of car-based tourist travel in Loch Lomond and Trossachs National Park, Scotland, *Tourism Management*, **29**, 561–580.

Debbage, K. (1991) Spatial behaviour in a Bahamian resort, *Annals of Tourism Research*, **18**(2), 251-268.

Dolnicar, S. and Grün, B. (2013) Validly measuring destination images in survey studies, *Journal of Travel Research*, **52** (1), 3-13.

Dolnicar, S. and Grün, B. (2007) Assessing analytical robustness in cross-cultural comparisons, *International Journal of Tourism, Culture, and Hospitality Research*, **1**(2), 140-160.

Flogenfeldt, T. (1999) Traveler geographic origin and market segmentation: the multi-trips destination case, *Journal of Travel and Tourism Marketing*, **8**(1), 111-118.

Forer, P.C. and Pearce, D. (1984) Spatial patterns of package tourism in New Zealand, *New Zealand Geographer*, **40**(1), 34-43.

Freytag, T. (2010) Déjà-vu: tourist practices of repeat visitors in the city of Paris, *Social Geography*, **5**(1), 49-58.

Goodman, L.A. (1963) Statistical methods for the preliminary analysis of transaction flows, *Econometrica*, **31**, 197-208.

Goodman, L.A. (1964) A short computer program for the analysis of transaction flows, *Behavorial Science*, **9**, 176-86.

Hardy, A. and Birenboim, A. and Wells, M. (2020) Using geoinformatics to assess tourist dispersal at the state level, *Annals of Tourism Research*, **82.**

Hardy, A. and Pearson, L. (2016) Determining sustainable tourism in regions, *Sustainability*, **8**(7), 660.

Huang, X and Wu, B. (2012) Intra-attraction tourist spatial-temporal behaviour patterns, *Tourism Geographies*, **14** (4), 1-21.

Lau, A.L.S. and McKercher, B. (2004) Exploration versus acquisition: A comparison of first-time and repeat visitors, *Journal of Travel Research*, **42**(3), 279–285.

Lau, A.L.S. and McKercher, B. (2006) Understanding tourist movement patterns in a destination: A GIS approach, *Tourism and Hospitality Research*, **7**(1), 39–49.

Lau, P., Koo, T. and Dwyer, L. (2017) Metrics to measure the geographic characteristics of tourism markets: An integrated approach based on Gini index decomposition. *Tourism Management*, **59**, 171-181.

Lew, A. and McKercher, B. (2006) Modeling tourist movements: a local destination analysis, *Annals of Tourism Research*, **33**(2), 403–423.

Masiero, L. and Zoltan, J. (2013) Tourists' intra-destination visits and transport mode: A bivariate model, *Annals of Tourism Research*, **43**, 529–546.

McKercher, B. and Lau, G. (2008) Movement patterns of tourists within a destination, *Tourism Geographies*, **10**(3), 355-374.

McKercher, B. and Lew, A. (2003), Distance decay and the impact of effective tourism exclusion zones on international travel flows, *Journal of Travel Research*, **42**(2), 159-165.

McKercher, B., Shoval, N., Ng, E. and Birenboim, A. (2012) First and repeat visitor behaviour: GPS tracking and GIS analysis in Hong Kong, *Tourism Geographies*, **14**(1), 147-161.

McKercher, B. and Zoltan, J. (2014). Tourists flows and spatial behavior. In A. A. Lew, M. C. Hall, & A. M. Williams (Eds.), *The Wiley Blackwell Companion to Tourism* (pp. 33–44). Malden: John Wiley & Sons.

Mings, R.C. and McHugh, K. (1992) The spatial configuration of travel to Yellowstone National Park, *Journal of Travel Research*, **30**(4), 38-46.

Oldendick R.W. (2012) Survey research ethics. In L. Gideon (Ed), *Handbook of Survey Methodology for the Social Sciences*. New York, NY: Springer.

Oppermann, M. (1992) Intranational tourist flows in Malaysia, *Annals of Tourism Research*, **19**, 482-500.

Oppermann, M. (1995) A model of travel itineraries, *Journal of Travel Research*, **33**(4), 57-61.

Shoval, N. and Isaacson, M. (2007) Tracking tourists in the digital age, *Annals of Tourism Research*, **34**(1), 141–159.

Shoval, N., McKercher, B., Ng, E. and Birenboim, A (2011) Hotel location and tourism activity in cities, *Annals of Tourism Research*, **38**(4), 1594-1612.

Tideswell, C. and Faulkner, B. (1999) Multidestination travel patterns of international visitors to Queensland, *Journal of Travel Research*, **37**(4), 364-374.

Williams, A. V. and Zelinsky, W. (1970). On some patterns in international tourist flows. *Economic Geography*, **46**(4), 549-567.

4 Tracking Using GPS Technology

What this chapter will cover:

- The development of GPS technology and its application to tourist tracking research.

- The possibility for applying this technique in a range of different tourism contexts.

- The detailed spatio-temporal findings regarding tourists' mobility, that have emerged from this technique.

- The challenges that GPS technology faces in terms of its limited application, battery life and requirement for outdoor environments.

- The considerations that researchers must take to use GPS research in and ethical manner.

Introduction

The use of global positioning system (GPS) technology underpins many different methods of tracking. GPS tracking involves the use of a beacon that sends the location of a device to satellites to determine the precise location of the beacon. In recent years, technological improvements have meant that GPS tracking units have become exponentially smaller in size. Whereas early portable beacons such as the Magellan (launched in 1989) were 22 cm in length and around 700 grams in weight, if not larger than television screens, they can now fit into the back of watches and mobile phones (Shoval and Isaacson, 2010). This chapter will explore the development of GPS technology and its application to tourism research, when utilised with portable GPS loggers.

Development of GPS technology

The desire to determine where humans are positioned relative to others and other objects is ancient, and dates back many millennia. This is evidenced through humans' alignment of buildings such as Stonehenge and the Pyramids relative to celestial constellations (Shoval and Isaacson, 2010; Hofmann-Wellenhoff, Lichtenegger and Collins, 2001). The development of GPS technology could be regarded as a modern extension of this desire. The technology involves a constellation of satellites that communicate with a device on the earth in order to triangulate the position of the device and deliver information on location and time (McKercher and Lau, 2009). The term Global Navigation Satellite Systems (GNSS) refers to these systems. GPS is one of these and was developed by the United States of America. Other systems include the Russian Global Navigation Satellite System (GLONASS), the Chinese BeiDou Navigation Satellite System and the European Union's Galileo system. Despite GNSS being the more accurate term, GPS technology is more commonly used as a generic term that refers to all systems, therefore will be used in this chapter.

GPS technology had its genesis in the 1950s and 1960s, following the launch of the first artificial earth satellite, Sputnik, in 1957. Sputnik led to the development of technology that could instantaneously determine precise locations anywhere in the world. Following this, in 1965, TRANSIT systems were developed by the United States military to assist submarines with navigation. TRANSIT used six satellites that orbited at 1100km altitude and allowed for the determination of the exact location of vessels and aircraft. However, the system was limited in its accuracy and ability to provide a continual position. Consequently, in the early 1970s, GPS was developed by the military to overcome these limitations, before being made available to civilians in the early 1980s (Shoval and Isaacson, 2010; Hofmann-Wellenhoff, Lichtenegger and Collins, 2001).

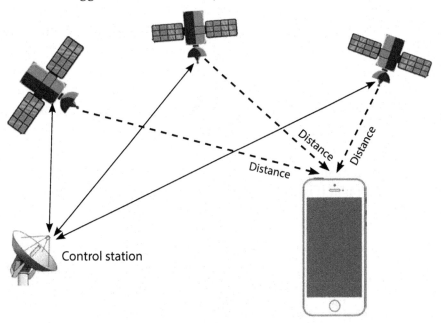

Distance

Distance

Distance

Control station

Figure 4.1: How GPS systems work. A network of control stations makes sure that satellites are always where they are supposed to be. The phone picks up signals from the satellites and calculates the distance from their known positions. As long as at least three satellites' signals can be picked up, the phone can calculate its position to within a few metres.

Today, GPS technology is embedded in many different devices. For the purposes of tourist tracking research, the most significant of these are GPS loggers and data pushers/GPS beacons. GPS loggers are made up of several components including a beacon, that transmits a signal to satellites and a logger that stores coordinate information at regular intervals inside the device. These coordinates can then be transferred via a memory card or USB port to a computer for analysis.

Data pushers/GPS beacons are used to track movement in real time. These devices push or send a signal with location details, at regular intervals, to a server where data can be stored and analysed immediately. Data pushers come in a range of formats from stand-alone tracking devices attached to rental cars or company assets (such as animals or aircraft), through to smart watches and mobile phones.

The GPS system was released for commercial and individual use in 1989, shortly after the development of the mobile phone, which was first developed in 1983 by Motorola (Seward, 2013). This resulted in many GPS devices being produced, whose sole capability was to track location and visualise it on a screen (Figure 4.1). Following this, technology enabled GPS loggers to be developed at a smaller size and as a result GPS capability was embedded into mobile phones – the first mobile phone with GPS capabilities was launched by Benefon in 1999 and since the mid-2000s, most mobile phones now have GPS capabilities. And most recently, the size of GPS units has reduced in size even further and smart watches with GPS functionality are now immensely popular (Figure 4.2).

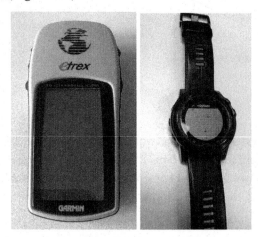

Figure 4.2: An early GPS unit designed for hiking and wayfinding in 2000 and a more recent smartphone watch with GPS capability, released around 2016.

Use of GPS for tracking

The use of GPS to track tourists' movement is commonly reported within tourism research literature. Early research most commonly asked participants to carry a GPS unit. Commonly, their location-based data was synced with survey data in order to gain insights into the factors associated with different movement patterns. Studies of this type have explored recreational users on trails in South Carolina (Beeco and Hallo, 2014; Hallo et al., 2012), recreational users in in Virginia (Beeco et al., 2013), tourists in Hong Kong (McKercher et al., 2012; Grinberger,

Shoval and McKercher, 2014); tourists in theme parks (Birenboim et al., 2013); tourists in cities (Edwards and Griffin, 2013; Modsching et al., 2008); at sports events (Pettersson and Zillinger, 2011); and on cruise ship tourists (De Cantis et al., 2018). More recently, participants with smart watches have been asked to track themselves and then share their data via sporting apps with researchers. This method is reported later in the book in Chapter 6.

Conceptual findings that have emerged from this technique

4

Many conceptual findings have emerged from studies that have tracked tourists' mobility using GPS technology. For example, McKercher et al. (2012) used GPS loggers to track independent tourists in Kowloon, Hong Kong for one day during their travels. They were asked to fill out a questionnaire to determine aspects including their total trip duration, travel party size, demographic profile and length of stay. The study confirmed existing research that first-time visitors tend to 'sample' destinations by wandering through it widely; in their case, this was on foot. They also demonstrated a propensity to visit iconic destinations and stay longer at them and a tendency to take longer day trips from the hotel. Conversely repeat visitors tended to concentrate their activities by visiting fewer places. The repeat visitor was more sporadic in their behaviour and had multiple forays from their hotel during the day.

Grinberger, Shoval and McKercher (2014) also made significant conceptual findings through their study that assessed the movement of tourists for one day in Hong Kong using GPS loggers. They assessed the impact of the internal decision-making process upon tourists' activity by looking at time-space constraints. They concluded that 'activity time' is a crucial factor that influences the spatial distribution of tourism activity and that three time-space strategies were employed by tourists. In descending order of total path length, these included:

- travel over large distances with few stops and longer time in stops;

- travel over medium distances with a higher number of longer stops; and

- travel over shorter distances with more time in a lower number of stops.

GPS technology has also resulted in better understanding of the impact that accommodation has upon tourists' mobility. Shoval et al. (2012) did a study in Hong Kong where the day trip behaviours of tourists were assessed. The authors noted that older tourism studies often disregarded hotel locations as a mitigating factor for behaviour. However, their study clearly demonstrated the impact of accommodation distance on tourist's behaviour in a variety of ways: they found it impacted upon behaviour as visitation was spatially concentrated around the hotel and that there was also evidence of diurnal concentration of visitation. This concept was referred to as the Distance Decay effect, whereby tourists' time budgets differed according to how far their hotel was located from attractions.

Urban research using GPS has also resulted in a greater understanding of how tourists move through cities. Edwards and Griffin (2013) used GPS loggers to explore how tourists moved through the cities of Melbourne and Sydney, Australia. The research tracked 154 groups for one day. At the end of the day the groups undertook a semi-structured interview and completed a questionnaire. The demographic data was then combined with the GPS data. The research demonstrated that understanding visitor movement is the first step in enhancing dispersal to ensure that benefits are dispersed more widely. The data provided visual maps that could inform those assisting tourists with planning and recommendations. It also illustrated where tourists were not dispersing, thus highlighting possibilities for where future tourism development could occur.

More recently, Sugimoto, Ota and Suzuki (2019) combined GPS logger data with survey data to explore the movement of 155 tourists from three train station locations in Tokyo, Japan, for one day. They found that the location of the train station where tourists were recruited had an important impact on how far tourists travelled. The study also illustrated that the spatial structure of urban environments (e.g. where train stations are located and where points of interest occur) clearly impacts visitors' movement. This study was able to determine that distance decay effect is still an important factor and that tourists tend to visit places that are close to railway stations, although a major attraction would also warrant longer periods of time being spent there. They also found that the experience of a visitor affects visitor mobility and that differentiation should be made between those who are frequent repeat visitors and those that are less frequent repeat visitors.

Theme parks, as a context, have also been explored using GPS. Birenboim et al. (2013) assessed family groups in a theme park in Catalonia. Families were tracked using a GPS logger for the duration of their one-day visit, and their tracks were integrated with a questionnaire. The results demonstrated that visitors tend to follow similar temporal patterns, in terms of length of visit, visitor time budgets, and diurnal and intra-diurnal patterns. The research demonstrated that these patterns remain similar across the seasons – strengthening the theory that tourists display very distinct activity rhythms.

Tourist mobility through historical locations has also been explored using GPS. Zheng, Huang and Li (2017) assessed tourists' movement through the Summer Palace in Beijing. Visitors were asked to carry a GPS unit that tracked movement every three minutes, and to fill out a questionnaire at the end of their day. 117 tourists were recruited. These researchers developed a predictive tool that was able to predict where tourists will travel, based upon their movement characteristics. Their heuristic prediction algorithm was designed for integration into apps and the authors argued it could play an important role in destination management and crowd control. The researchers also recognised the potential for strengthening the approach by factoring in tourists' demographic characteristics when creating the predictions.

East et al. (2017) also used GPS to explore theme parks visitors' movement. Their study tracked 931 visitors for one day, in a zoo in Hampshire, UK, using a survey combined with GPS loggers. The study demonstrated that the group type, repeat vs first time visitation, and the distance that was travelled within the park, had a large impact on how much time visitors spent at specific locations within the park.

The context of cruise ships has also provided insights into tourists' behaviour. De Cantis et al. (2016) surveyed cruise ship passengers before and after their day trip and asked them to carry GPS loggers that tracked their movement in Palermo, Sicily. They tracked 322 tourists, some who had purchased a tour by the cruise company and some who planned to travel independently. Their study yielded significant data on tourists' movement through time and space that was useful for destination managers as it showed where crowding occurred, and where services were over-used or under-utilised. The results also demonstrated that socio-demographic characteristics such as age, income and education level were related to mobility – in this study, older people with lower income and lower levels of education were found to display lower levels of mobility whilst off the ship.

In further cruise ship tourism research in Palermo (using the same data as the aforementioned study) and Dubrovnik (where only independent cruise ship passengers were sampled), Ferrante, De Cantis and Shoval (2018) conducted pre and post day trip surveys and asked cruise ship passengers to carry a GPS logger for the day. The study produced a replicable methodology, that determines the way in which different segments of cruise ship passengers travel through cruise ship destinations. They determined that cruise ship passengers behave differently in differing destinations; this is where the potential lies for destinations to use the methodology themselves, as the knowledge they provide will influence travel behaviour. The research showed that those with higher income and education levels aged between 36 and 55 will seek what can be described as:

> '...intense experiences of the destination, in terms of time spent offshore, places visited, and transportation mode. On the contrary, younger and senior cruise ship passengers with lower levels of education and a lower income, will make a shorter visit at the destination, concentrating their activities on places adjacent to the port area.' (Ferrante, De Cantis and Shoval (2018, p. 1444).

These results present opportunities for segment product offerings that cater to different types of passengers.

Beeco et al. (2012) tracked 490 tourists in Floyd and Patrick Counties, USA, for two days to determine how psychological factors influenced travel behaviours. Their research found that the dichotomous differentiation of wanderer and planner segments were not as different as those posited by McKercher, Wong and Lau (2006). The researchers identified a third group, Ambivalent Travellers, who did not like to wander or plan. They found that the major difference between wanders and planners was their propensity to make pre-trip plans, but that the groups did not differ in terms of where they went. So, the authors proposed that while they have different styles of travel, they behaved in similar ways, both spatially and temporally. The authors noted the limitations of GPS – since they found that movement is not the defining aspect that differentiates wanderers and planners, the GPS approach may have overlooked other affective differences, as it is unable to explore all aspects of behaviour.

In further research conducted in natural areas, Meijles et al. (2014) tracked 138 tourists in the Drents-Friese Wold National Park, Netherlands, for one day. This data was synced with a questionnaire that visitors were asked to complete. They found that although many groups tended to stay in the park for around the same time, the distance they walked varied. Specifically, larger groups and those with children walked shorter distances. They also found the motivation to visit the park (e.g. to walk versus to socialise) was associated with the speed at which the group travelled – socialisers were the slowest walkers.

In summary, some of the most important conceptual findings to emerge from the use of GPS include:

- **Influencers of travel patterns:** Beeco and Hallo (2014), plus East et al. (2017) found that knowledge of destination, the personal characteristics of tourists, and activity type influenced tourists' spatial travel patterns.

- **Significant influence that knowledge of destination has upon spatial patterns of behaviour:** the experience of a visitor, such as whether they are a first or repeat visitor was found to be significant by both McKercher et al, (2012) and Sugimoto et al. (2019).

- **Influence of time on spatial travel patterns:** Grinberger, Shoval and McKercher (2014) found that activity time has a major influence on spatial distribution of tourism activity.

- **Influence of hotel on distance travel:** Shoval et al. (2011) found that hotel location impacted behaviour temporally and spatially.

Methodological studies using GPS data

In addition to conceptual advances, researchers have explored the efficacy of this form of location-based data gathering in terms of its palatability to research participants, the quality of data when using different GPS loggers, and the impact of the use of cleaned versus un-cleaned data. Hallo et al. (2012) compared two newly released GPS loggers with an older style device to decipher whether the data they produced was significantly different. They collected data over four days to minimise the effects of atmospheric disturbances. The precision of each of the devices was then compared, with the average data point variance at each location used as the measure of precision. They also assessed how the units performed in the field, along a trail in South Carolina and in the Cascade Mountains of Washington. The researchers were interested in whether the GPS units tracked a route that deviated from the actual trail, how the battery life performed and the cost of the units. They found that while every unit performed differently in terms of data precision, in dense forests the new devices performed far more effectively. They did note that while all systems performed well down to minus 10 degrees Celsius, two of the three systems were not waterproof.

The authors also assessed participants' willingness to participate in research that utilised GPS loggers. They randomly selected visitors to take part in the research and asked them to carry a GPS unit for the duration of their stay in the Blue Ridge Parkway and the Floyd and Patrick Counties, USA. 65.8% agreed to take part and 96.9% of these participants returned the GPS units that they had carried. Finally, in further methodological research in natural areas in the United States,

Beeco and Hallo (2014) compared the differences between cleaned and uncleaned data – in their case they found that uncleaned data reported longer total distance travelled.

Advantages of GPS technology

The use of GPS loggers as a method to collect location-based data has many advantages. These advantages relate to their physical appearance and their ability to garner high resolution data. With regards to their physical appearance, GPS loggers are small devices – at the time of writing many were only around 5cms in length and 3cms in width. This portability and unobtrusive size mean they can be easily carried by participants while travelling (McKercher and Lau, 2009).

A further advantage is the highly accurate data that GPS loggers can produce. It is now commonplace for GPS loggers to have the ability to track to within 1m of accuracy (McKercher and Lau, 2009; Yun and Park, 2015). The data produced from these devices is continuous and includes speed and directionality. If combined with surveys, this data can provide detailed insights into different tourist segments' behaviour (Asakura and Iryo, 2007; O'Connor, Zerger and Itami, 2005). GPS logger data is of a far greater accuracy and resolution than data that can be collected through surveys or travel diaries (Edwards et al., 2010).

Ethical consent is also a major positive aspect of this approach. Data loggers are easily visible, so participants are most likely to be fully aware of their function. This ensures that consent is gained, and that tracking is not conducted covertly and, therefore, illegally.

Limitations of GPS technology

Despite its advantages, there are a variety of limitations to the use of GPS technology. First, GPS data alone tells analysts precisely where individuals go with great accuracy, but unless combined with surveys, nothing is known about the characteristics of the tourists using the logger. GPS data alone does not allow an understanding of preferences, behavioural segments, the impact of prior travel experience on movement or the motivation of travellers. This richness in data may only be achieved when the technique is combined with survey research that is synced with individuals' location-based data. GPS trackers alone are unable to capture in-situ, experiential data.

GPS data is also limited to studies that seek to track movement outdoors. GPS signals rely on a GPS receiver having exposure to the sky and orbiting satellites. GPS does not perform well indoors as direct exposure to satellites is not often possible under roof spaces. Poor weather conditions such as humidity and geographical factors such as heavily forested areas can also interrupt the signal and produce errors (often referred to as 'noise') in the data, leading to imprecise readings.

A further data error is referred to as a 'multipath error' – this occurs in high density urban areas, where housing, particularly close-density housing, can interrupt the signal, causing it to deflect off the objects on the way from the satellite to the receiver (Hofmann-Wellenhof, Lichtenegger, Collins, 2001; Pettersson and Zillinger, 2011; McKercher and Lau, 2009). However, this issue is not insurmountable; Pettersson and Zillinger (2011) demonstrated that multipath errors can be iden-tified and overcome when there is an obviously incorrect point that does not correlate with previous or subsequent time and space points. Overall, however, as the efficacy of GPS is diminished in indoor envi-ronments and for urban tourist destinations, it means that the accuracy of tourism research relying on GPS can, at times, be compromised (Shoval and Isaacson, 2010; McKercher and Lau 2009).

Further limitations have been raised because of the physical presence of GPS loggers. While a distinct advantage is that their physical presence helps to ensure that participants are aware they are being tracked, it has also been argued that the knowledge that one is being tracked could result in participants changing their behaviour (Winters et al., 2008). It has also been noted that as the use of GPS loggers is a participatory method, there is a risk that self-selection bias exists, whereby individu-als with certain characteristics would be more likely to be involved in studies using that method and therefore, could be over-represented in the sample (Versichele et al., 2014). Moreover, previous studies that have used these devices have only been conducted for one day at most.

It remains unknown whether participants would be willing to carry them for multiple days at a time.

Shoval et al. (2014) explored the use of GPS by geographers. They argued that while GPS has been used to track the movement of tourists, geography as a discipline has been slow to use GPS to collect data. This may be in part due to the critique of the method voiced by critical geographers that GPS traces movement but overlooks participants' subjectivities and is, as a consequence, too focused on physical movement alone (Gren, 2001).

The immense detail that GPS loggers can provide in terms of tourists' movement means that a large amount of data is produced. Beeco and Hallo (2014) suggest that this can be a potential limitation to the use of GPS and that as a result, researchers must play a balancing act between collecting enough data to be able to track tourists' movement, while not collecting so much data that it becomes unworkable. In their case, they found that 15 second intervals were suitable for hikers, mountain bikers, horse riders and runners.

There are also issues that can arise when cleaning the data. Meijles et al. (2014) argued that data cleaning and the removal of errors can be very time consuming, thus presenting a major disadvantage of this approach. They called for the development of algorithms for cleaning to assist this process, but cautioned that they must be carefully thought through. This is discussed in Chapter 9.

Finally, there are concerns about the costs of this form of research. Loggers range from US $50 to upwards of $250 so if they are required for samples of large numbers of people, GPS research is very expensive to run, despite not necessarily having to be all used simultaneously (Shoval et al., 2014). Due to the cost involved in purchasing loggers, many studies request that participants return the device at the end of the study period. This may result in the loss of some devices. High costs associated with studies of this nature has meant much of the existing research has only used small sample sizes as the cost of scaling up is too prohibitive. They also differ widely in their quality of data collection, ability to withstand weather conditions such as rain, price, and battery life (Hallo et al., 2012).

Ethical considerations of this approach

The act of asking a potential participant to carry a physical device such as a GPS logger means that the goal of collecting data is harder to conceal. However, ethical research using this technique needs to do more than gain consent from participants to carry a GPS logger. Many jurisdictions are now guided by University and/or National Ethical Guidelines. Taking the Australian Government and Universities *National Statement on Ethical Conduct in Human Research* (Commonwealth of Australia, 2018) as an example, participants

- Must not be coerced to take part in research;

- Must be made aware of what the study involves;

- Must be invited to opt in rather than opt out;

- Must be able to withdraw from the study at any time (including the withdrawal of their data) without effect;

- Must be made aware of how their data will be used, how it will be stored, and for how long the data will be used and by whom;

- Must be made aware whether their participation will be anonymous, confidential or whether their identity will be revealed;

- Must be made aware of the risks, if any, of being involved; and

- Must be given the opportunity to be given feedback on the results of the study.

Despite early concerns about the potential for GPS studies to violate personal privacy, the physical presence of the logger, which must be given to participants to carry, means that covert tracking is not a major issue with this method. Provided researchers respect their country, regional and institutional ethical requirements for informed consent, the ethical issues raised by this approach should be minimal.

Summary

The use of GPS loggers is commonly used in tourism tracking studies due to the highly detailed data that it can produce. It is a particularly strong method when used for one day – this is often the optimal time for the battery life of the devices. As a result of the use of GPS technology, a variety of conceptual insights into the ways in which tourists travel have emerged. These include, but are not limited to, the difference in behaviour between first and repeat tourists (McKercher et al., 2012), the role of activity time in behaviour and a resultant theory on time-space strategies (Grinberger, Shoval and McKercher, 2014), the role of the hotel location (Shoval et al., 2011) and train station locations in determining travel behaviour (Sugimoto, Ota and Suzuki, 2019), and the presence of temporal and spatial activity rhythms amongst tourists (Birenboim et al., 2013).

However, there are limitations to this method. Battery life has limited the application largely to one day, it is expensive, and its application is limited to outdoor areas, with performance being compromised in highly urbanised or forested areas. In order to understand the impact of the traveller demographics or travel history on behaviour, GPS data from loggers must be synced with survey data, which requires time and synthesis. This, combined with the extremely rich and large amounts of data that can be produced from loggers, can mean that data cleaning and analysis can be a lengthy process.

However, despite these limitations, this method is particularly useful for projects that seek to understand highly detailed movement of tourists over a short period of time in outdoor environments.

4

Key learnings from this chapter:

- The application of GPS technology has resulted in highly detailed spatio-temporal insights into tourists' behaviour.

- GPS research has resulted in insights regarding tourists behaviour in cities, the impact of hotel location and destination familiarity on tourists' movement, and visitor movement patterns.

- GPS loggers are limited by their short battery life, functionality that is limited to the outdoors and inability to collect socio-demographic data.

- The non-covert manner of GPS research means that informed consent can be gained from participants.

References

Asakura, Y. and Iryo, T. (2007) Analysis of tourist behaviour based on the tracking data collected using mobile communication instrument, *Transportation Research Part A: Policy and Practice*, **41**(7), 684–690.

Beeco, J.A. and Hallo, J. (2014) GPS tracking of visitor use: factors influencing visitor spatial behaviour on a complex trail system', *Journal of Park and Recreation Administration*, **32**(2), 43-61.

Beeco, J., Huang, W., Hallo, J., Norman, W.C,. McGehee, N., McGee, J. and Goetcheus, C. (2013) GPS tracking of travel routes of wanderers and planners, *Tourism Geographies*, **15**(3), 551-573.

Birenboim, A., Anton-Clavé, S., Paolo, Russo, A., Shoval, N. (2013) Temporal activity patterns of theme park visitors, *Tourism Geographies*, **15**(4), 601-619.

Commonwealth of Australia (2018) *National Statement on Ethical Conduct in Human Research*. National Health and Medical Research Council, Australian Research Council and Universities Australia. Available from https://www.nhmrc.gov.au/about-us/publications/national-statement-ethical-conduct-human-research-2007-updated-2018 [Accessed 27th August 2019].

De Cantis, S., Ferrante, M., Kahani, A. and Shoval, N. (2016) Cruise passengers' behavior at the destination: Investigation using GPS technology, *Tourism Management*, **52**, 133-150.

East, D., Osborne, P., Kemp, S. and Woodfine, T. (2017) Combining GPS & survey data improves understanding of visitor behaviour, *Tourism Management*, **61**, 307-320.

Edwards, D., Dickson, T., Griffin, .A, and Hayllar, B.(2010) Tracking the urban visitor: Methods for examining tourists' spatial behaviour and visual representations. In: Richard, G, Munsters (eds) *Cultural Tourism Research Methods*, CABI Publishing, Oxford, pp. 104-114.

Edwards, E. and Griffin, T. (2013) Understanding tourists' spatial behaviour: GPS tracking as an aid to sustainable destination management, *Journal of Sustainable Tourism*, **21**(4), 580-595.

Ferrante, M., De Cantis, S. and Shoval, N. (2018) A general framework for collecting and analysing the tracking data of cruise passengers at the destination, *Current Issues in Tourism*, **21**(12), 1426-1451.

Gren, M. (2001) Time geography matters. In: J. May, and N. Thrift(eds) *Timespace: Geographies of Temporality*. Routledge, London and New York, pp 208-225

Grinberger, Y., Shoval, N., McKercher, B. (2014) Typologies of tourists' time-space consumption: a new approach using GPS data and GIS tools, *Tourism Geographies*, **16**(1), 105-123.

Hallo, J., Beeco, A., Goetcheus, C., McGee, J., McGehee, N. and Norman, W. (2012) GPS as a method for assessing spatial and temporal use distributions of nature-based tourists, *Journal of Travel Research*, **51**(5), 591-606.

Hofmann-Wellenhof, B., Lichtenegger, H., Collins, J., (2001) *Global Positioning System: Theory and Practice*, 5th edn, New York: Springer Wien.

Meijles, E., de Bakker, M., Groote, P., and Barske, R. (2014) Analysing hiker movement patterns using GPS data: Implications for park management, *Computers, Environment and Urban Systems*, 44-57.

McKercher, B. and Lau, G. (2009) Methodological considerations when mapping tourist movements in a destination, *Tourism Analysis*, **14**(4), 443-455.

McKercher , B. Shoval , N. Ng, E. and Birenboim, A. (2012) First and repeat visitor behaviour: GPS tracking and GIS analysis in Hong Kong, *Tourism Geographies*, **14**(1), 147-161

McKercher, B. and Wong and Lau, G. (2006) How tourists consume a destination, *Journal of Business Research*, **59**(5), 647-652.

Modsching, M., Kramer, R., Hagen, K.T. and Gretzel, U. (2008) Using location-based tracking data to analyze the movements of city tourists, *Information Technology & Tourism*, **10**(1), 31–42.

O'Connor, A., Zerger, A. and Itami, B. (2005) Geo-temporal tracking and analysis of tourist movement, *Mathematics and Computers in Simulation*, **69**(1/2), 135–150.

Pettersson, R. and Zillinger, M. (2011) Time and space in event behaviour: Tracking visitors by GPS, *Tourism Geographies*, **13**, 1-20.

Shoval, N. and Isaacson, M. (2010) *Tourist Mobility and Advanced Tracking Technologies*, New York: Routledge.

Shoval, N., Kwan, M, Reinau, K, Harder, H (2014) The shoemaker's son always goes barefoot: Implementation of GPS and other tracking technologies for geographic research, *Geoforum* **51**(1), 1-5.

Shoval, N., McKercher, B., Ng, E., Birenboim, A. (2011) Hotel location and tourism activity in cities. *Annals of Tourism Research*, **38**(4), 1594-1612.

Sugimoto, K., Ota, K., and Suzuki, S. (2019) Visitor mobility and spatial structure in a local urban tourism destination: GPS tracking and network analysis, *Sustainability*,**11**(3), 919.

Seward, Z. (2013) The first mobile phone call was made 40 years ago today, *The Atlantic*, https://www.theatlantic.com/technology/archive/2013/04/the-first-mobile-phone-call-was-made-40-years-ago-today/274611/ [Accessed 5th July 2020]

Versichele, M., de Groote, L., Bouuaert, M., Neutens, T., Moerman, I., Van d Weghe, I. (2014) Pattern mining in tourist attraction visits through association rule learning on Bluetooth tracking data: A case study of Ghent, Belgium, *Tourism Management*, **22**, 67-81.

Winters, P. Brabeua, S., Georggi, N. (2008) Smart phone application to influence travel behaviours (TRAC-IT Phase 3) (Report no. 549-35).

Yun, H. and Park, M. (2015) Time-space movement of festival visitors in rural areas using a smart phone application, *Asia Pacific Journal of Tourism Research*, **20**(11), 1246-1265.

Zheng, W., Huang, X. and Li, Y. (2017) Understanding the tourist mobility using GPS: Where is the next place?, *Tourism Management*, **59**, 267-280.

5 Tracking via Geotagged Social Media Data

What this chapter will cover:

- How geotagged social media data offers researchers the opportunity to collect vast amounts of big data from some, but not all, social media platforms.

- The variety of methods that can be employed to obtain geotagged social media data.

- The range of conceptual insights that have emerged from this cost efficient and reliable form of data.

- That the non-covert manner of this form of research requires careful steps to ensure individuals' data is treated in an ethical manner.

Introduction

Over the past twenty years, social media has changed the ways in which we plan, travel and reflect on our travels. Tourists use social media while travelling to stay in touch with friends and family, enhance their social status (Guo et al., 2015); and assist others with decision making (Xiang and Gretzel, 2010; Yoo and Gretzel, 2010). They also use it to report back to their friends and family where they are. This can be done using a geotag function that provides a location for where a post is made. While little is known about why tourists choose to geotag their social media posts, Chung and Lee (2016) suggest that geotags may be used in an altruistic manner by tourists, in order to provide information, and because they elicit a sense of anticipated reward. What is known, however, is that the function offers researchers the ability to understand where tourists travel.

There are two types of geotagged social media data. The first of these is discussed in this chapter and may be defined as single point geo-referenced data – geotagged social media posts whose release is chosen by the user. This includes data gathered from social media apps such as Facebook, Instagram, Twitter and WeiChat. The method of obtaining this data involves the collation of large numbers of discrete geotagged updates or photographs. Data can be collated via an application programming interface (API) provided by the app developer to researchers, by automated data scraping via computer programs, perhaps written in Python, or manually by researchers. The second type of data is continuous location-based data from applications that are designed to track movement constantly, such as Strava or MyFitnessPal. Tracking methods using this continuous location-based data are discussed in detail in the following chapter.

Geotagged social media data can provide rich information for planners and tourism managers, as well as for tourists (Garcia-Palomores, Gutierrez and Minguez, 2015). The use of data from this source is often referred to as crowd sourcing, digital foot printing, or data crawling (Mukhina, Rakitin and Vishertin, 2017). It is an extremely useful tool to indicate the level of attractiveness – or unattractiveness – of different spaces (Kachkaev and Wood, 2013). Further, it can be done in real time. However, it may also be regarded as a fast-moving method that is subject to ethical constraints and constraints related to platforms' terms and conditions. This chapter will review this method, its application within tourism, and the ethical and legal considerations that are associated with this technique.

Using crowd sourced geotagging to track tourist mobility

In the past ten years, there has been an explosion of publicly available geotagged social media data on the internet, as a result of apps offering the geotagging functionality to its users. Facebook, Instagram, Snapchat and Twitter are examples of social media apps that offer this functionality. Geotagging is defined as a process whereby geospatial information, temporal information, and/or textual information is added to online content such as written posts or photographs (Dickinger et al., 2008; Kádár and Gede, 2013; Wong, Law, Li, 2017). This is possible because individuals' devices (mobile phone, computer or tablet) add their location to text, photographs or documents – and this can be done manually by the user each time they post, or automatically via their settings within the app (Dickinger et al., 2008). The majority of research in this space has focussed on geotagged photographs or text, but research that assesses geotags can include articles and video content.

As mentioned earlier, the use of data produced through web-based platforms is often referred to as crowdsourcing. Crowdsourced data has been defined by Walden-Schreiner et al. (2018: 782) as:

> '... information that is generated by many individuals, often accessed through web platforms'. Data generated from this method can include '... geotagged photos shared publicly on social-media and other social-media-derived sources of volunteered geographic information (i.e., GPS tracks).'

Since its early use by authors such as Girardin et al. (2008), the collation of geotags as a tool to explore tourism behaviour has emerged as a significant method through which tourist mobility and behaviour may be understood (Walden-Schreiner et al., 2018). Data sourced using this method can also assess the economic impact of tourism (Sonter et al., 2016) and tourists' preferences for biodiversity (Hausmann et al., 2017). Ironically, despite its enormous potential, Wong, Law and Li (2017: 48) describe the field as being in the 'nascent stage' with the majority of research being published in the information technology or computer science field.

5

Specifically, the analysis of this form of data involves either:

1. Collating a sequence of geotags produced by individuals via their social media account, in order to understand how tourists move sequentially through destinations; or

2. Assessing geotags in a single location to assess crowding and usage.

Both these analytical methods involve gathering data from social media apps such as Facebook, Instagram, Twitter and WeChat via the collation of large numbers of discrete geotagged updates or photographs. This data can be gathered in three ways.

- The first is via an API provided by the app developer to researchers. An API is a feature that allows data from an application such as a social media platform to be accessed. This feature allows researchers to access data relevant to their study.

- The second means by which this data may be collated is via data scraping that automatically gathers data that is relevant to the study region, topic and timeframe, via computer script written in a language such as python. The process of scraping may be done automatically only if the User Agreement of the social media platforms allows the practice.

- The third option for these platforms is to scrape the data manually, using copy and paste functions, where the photograph of the post, the text accompanying it and accompanying "@" and hashtags are collected, for specific geo-located places, in specific time frames.

Figure 5.1: Apps that have been used for geo-tagged social media tracking: Facebook, Instagram, Twitter and Flickr

Geotagged social media data can be analysed in a number of ways. Texts, hashtags, and the use of linking posts with other sites through the use of "@" can be analysed quantitatively (Rossi et al., 2018) or qualitatively (Gretzel and Hardy, 2019). Images can be analysed for their content and geotags can also be analysed in order to determine the frequency of visitation to certain locations. In addition to assessing concentration of tourists at sites, social media geotags can also be used to assess movement through time and space, when users' movements are tracked individually. This technique can be used to ascertain sequential movement patterns of individual tourists between different sites (Jiang et al., 2011; Zheng et al., 2012). Wong, Law and Li (2017) argue that this information is very useful for tourism suppliers, including travel agents and destination management organizations, as they can indicate hot spots, overuse and underuse. It is also useful for protected area managers; Walden-Schreiner et al. (2018) assessed temporal and spatial movement in protected areas using this data and found seasonal variations in park use with implications for infrastructure use.

5

Figure 5.2: An example of a geo-tagged social media post, displaying the location of where the post was made.

The ubiquitous use of social media has led to suggestions that tracking tourists' movement through social media geotags can be a proxy for actual visitation numbers (Levin et al., 2015; Spalding et al., 2017; Walden-Schreiner et al., 2018). For example, Kádár (2014) used Flickr data from 2011 in Prague, Budapest and Vienna and compared the numbers of photos with statistics for the cities. The correlation coefficient between tourist bed nights, arrival numbers and number of photographs was 0.92; thus they argued the correlation proved the reliability of the data for estimating usage. In a further study, Tenkanen et al. (2017) compared data from Instagram, Twitter and Flickr and assessed how the parks popularity and visitors counts compared with visitor statistics. They found that:

- There were synergies between the amount of posts and popularity of parks and actual visitation.

- The accuracy of determining popularity of parks through social media posts decreases with the popularity of parks – in their study the top four posts from Instagram was the same as the top four in terms of visitor statistics. But social media posts underestimated the popularity of the less visited parks.

- They found that the seasonality of park visitation was also reflected in the social media posts.

- Instagram was twice as reliable compared to Twitter and Flickr. This difference was less evident in South Africa though, thus indicating that different countries favour different social media platforms.

Conceptual findings that have emerged from geotagged social media data

In the short time that this method has been available to tourism researchers, it has significantly enriched our understandings of how tourists behave (Garcia-Palomores, Gutierrez and Minguez, 2015). The following sections explore how different social media platforms have been utilised.

Twitter

Research into the activity and movement of different tourists has rarely been conducted via Twitter, but of those studies that have, a variety of interesting findings have emerged. Ramasco (2016) ranked tourist sites' attractiveness according to tourists' place of residence and Hawelka et al. (2014) assessed the volume of international travel using data from users' country of residence. The authors suggested that geo-located Twitter data may be considered as proxy for mobility of humans, particularly in studies exploring country-to-country flows. Chua et al. (2016) used geotagged Twitter data to assess users flows in Cilento, Italy. They undertook trajectory mining, whereby they did a time-ordered collection of data that would trace the movement of a person through space and time. The pathways revealed the sequence of movement from one location to the next and across seasons, and in doing so determined distinct differences between how domestic and international tourists move through the region.

Flickr

Flickr, a social media site based on photography, is also a rich source of data. The platform has been interrogated by many researchers in order to determine intensity of use in different spaces, as well as frequency of visitation over different seasons (Popescu, Grefenstette, and Moëllic, 2009). User profiling has also been conducted using the semantics of users to determine their behaviour (Popescu, Grefenstette, and Moëllic, 2009). Gavric et al. (2011) also applied CommonGIS, a Java-based tool to images in Flickr in Berlin to assess the popularity of tourist sites. Flickr has also been used to compare domestic and international tourists behaviour in Zurich (Straumann, Çöltekin and Andrienko, 2014), and to estimate length of stay in cities, with the accuracy of the estimation being proven to be quite high (Koerbitz, Önder, and Hubmann-Haidvogel, 2013).

Vu et al. (2015) assessed geotagged photographs on Flickr of 2,100 tourists to Hong Kong. They used the Flickr API to obtain the data but noted it was limited because it does not identify owners (thus one user could add 400 photos and each would be regarded as being created by a different user), plus they could be taken in transit. The researchers identified owner IDs to determine who took certain photographs and also identified residents by extracting their country of origin via the Flickr search function. The authors then used the Markov Chain method to do travel pattern mining – a process that determines travel patterns and routes taken by tourists between key attractions. They were then able to determine flows of movement between attractions and tendencies to travel to places at different times, according to country of origin. For example they found that Asian tourists tended to arrive in Hong Kong during the day (10am – 5pm) whereas Western tourists tended to arrive at any time. They also determined that Hong Kong central was most commonly visited by Asians between 11am and 4pm, whereas the busiest time for Western visitors was 3pm.

Girardin et al. (2008) demonstrated the different digital footprints between locals and tourists, using Flickr. They classified tourists as those in Rome who took all their photographs within a 30 day period. They triangulated their assumption by looking at the data attached to Flickr users' accounts that suggested where they were from. They determined digital desire lines – people's paths through the city, using the time stamp of photographs. They also assessed their tags and how photographers described these places. This research demonstrated the potential for geographically referenced digital footprints.

Panoramio

Garcia-Palomores, Gutierrez, and Minguez (2015) assessed the now defunct website Panoramio. They mapped the intensity of photographs from different tourist sites in cities and explored the differences between tourists and locals. Beyond Panoramio, the authors suggested that this technique can be used to assess carrying capacity and assess distribution across cities. They also suggested its potential in assessing new potential tourism sites, such as accommodation and information services, and its applicability for marketing agencies and planners, as it reveals under- and over-used sites (Garcia-Palomores, Gutierrez, and Minguez, 2015). Zhou et al. (2014) developed categories of the attributes of a city according to photographs derived from Panoramio. They identified different dimensions including green space, architecture, transportation, and activity and assessed the visual similarity of many cities.

Tammet, Luberg and Järv (2013) have developed Sightsmap (www. sightsmap.com) that consolidates all Panoramio, Wikipedia and Foursquare photographs, so that viewers can see the most popular sites around the world. Similarly Eric Fisher via Flickr, has created The Geotaggers' World Atlas, which consolidates data from many major cities around the world.

While many studies have used only one platform, Salas-Olmedo et al. (2018) compared geolocated data from the Panoramio platform; Foursquare and Twitter. They assessed the number of photos and tweets and the density of tourists for each of the three platforms to try and mitigate user bias associated with each of the different platforms.

Other platforms

A variety of other social media platforms have been used to track the mobility of tourists, albeit in varying degrees. Despite Facebook's size, the strict terms and conditions placed on the use of individuals' data and a lack of an easily accessible API has prevented mobility researchers from using its data. The difficulty of using this platform was noted by Tenkanen et al. (2017). Similarly, Facebook's other company, Instagram, has the same terms and conditions regarding the use of its data. Prior to the implementation of these strict terms, some automated scraping (using process mining techniques) was conducted by Diamantini et al. (2017) to assess the mobility patterns of Instagram users at EXPO 2015. Another social media app, Foursquare, has been used by Salas-Olmedo et al. (2018) to track tourists' mobility, using 'check-ins' as digital traces of mobility. Trip Advisor has also been used; van der Zee et al. (2020) used user generated content from the platform (sourced through manual coding) to reveal the digital footprints of tourists in five Flemish cities. Cristina and Stoleriu (2020) also used Trip Advisor data (sourced manually) to understand which destinations and attractions were appealing to tourists to Romania.

Tourist mobility has also been explored using the gigantic app, WeChat – now used by over a billion people. Experimental research was conducted by Gou et al. (2016) which determined its applicability. WeChat recently launched Mini Programs, an application that individuals can use without having to download or install. This offers

5

opportunities for tourist mobility to be tracked, as APIs are not available to researchers, although careful consideration is required to ensure data collected via Mini Programs is done so ethically.

Methodological findings that have emerged from geotagged social media data

One of the challenges with geotagged social media data is that it does not utilise survey data, therefore the researcher must determine whether each individual post that is being examined is that of a tourist, a business owner, or a local person. This technique was explored by Mukhina, Rakitin and Vishertin (2017) who assessed Instagram posts and proposed a method to separate locals and tourists, plus a method to classify places that are popular amongst locals. They concluded that, in their case study region, an Instagram user could be regarded as a tourist if:

- They did not have Saint Petersburg set as their home location; and

- Their posts from Saint Petersburg occurred within a 15 day window and, if applicable, were separated between windows by at least 30 days.

The 15 days was chosen because the Eurostat data suggested that 87% of outbound vacations by Europeans did not exceed 14 days (Figure 5.3).

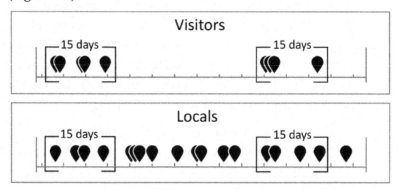

Figure 5.3: A time window strategy for tourists' movement through Saint Petersburg, (adapted from Mukhina, Rakitin and Vishertin, 2017: 2380)

The authors' criteria for determining who was a local included:

- The username states that the user is located in Saint Petersburg; and

- Posts were made over a period of time that exceeded 15 days.

The authors found that in the quiet seasons, there were many similarities between tourists' and locals' profiles; in the case of their research, most visitation and posting to Saint Petersburg was on the weekend. During the summer months, however, posts differed in terms of content and the time of day they were posted. However, they did note that the strategy of separating tourists from locals had limitations; if someone visited a city repeatedly with short stays, then they could accidentally be regarded as a local. Similarly, tourists who stay a long time could be regarded as locals. Moreover, a tourist who stays in the study location but takes photos outside of the city, could also confuse the data set.

A temporal dimension to differentiate tourists and locals was also used by Salas-Olmedo et al. (2018), who used data from Panoramio, Foursquare and Twitter concurrently, and defined residents as those who posted photos from a study region over a period of time greater than one week per year; less than one week was taken to mean tourists.

Salas-Olmedo et al. (2018) also argued that it is too selective to only use one data source to assess tourists movement; they used different social media outlets at different places. For example, they argued that some places don't allow photos (thus Instagram could not be used, but Twitter would be allowed) – this could create the potential for researchers to conclude that there were few visitors, if only one platform was used as a data source, when in fact there were many.

The same authors also assessed how different platforms performed, the biases that can emerge from each of three platforms they studied, and the impact of this for understanding tourist behaviour (Salas-Olmedo et al., 2018). They compared the digital footprints of three forms of tourists:

- Photographs that were geolocated on the Panoramio platform;

- Foursquare check-in data (to assess consumption); and

- Twitter for social commentary.

Their assessment quantified the number of photos and tweets as well as the density of tourists. They found that Twitter correlated well with accommodation – posts tended to occur at night time between 6pm and 10pm – possibly when tourists could access Wi-Fi. Thus, they argued Twitter data could present an accurate proxy for accommodation. Conversely, they found that Foursquare was commonly used at places related to consumption – attractions, restaurants, shopping, plus historic areas. Consequently, Foursquare data could be used as a good proxy for consumption.

Advantages with social media apps

One of the most obvious advantages of undertaking analysis using geotagged social media apps is the large amount of data that can be accessed (Wong, Law and Li, 2017). This technique can collate vast amounts of data in a small amount of time and at low cost, if automation is able to be employed. Moreover, if there is a sequence of geotagged photos provided by individuals, this technique can provide spatiotemporal data (Wong, Law and Li, 2017; Jiang et al., 2011; Zheng et al., 2012). It can also identify tourist preferences (Kisilevich et al., 2013) and therefore is very useful for destination marketing agencies, tourism businesses, and tourism planners. Arguably, because this technique involves the scraping of individual's data, it is also non-intrusive, as research subjects are not required to fill out surveys, install apps, or complete travel diaries (Straumann, Çöltekin and Andrienko, 2014).

Limitations with geotagged social media data

There are, as with all data that seeks to track movement, several limitations with the use of geotagged social media data. Tenkanen et al. (2017) argue that one of these is the tendency of research to focus on one platform at a time. This can introduce biases as different social media platforms attract different types of users. There is also an issue related to sampling bias as not all tourists take, share, and geo-tag photos (Richards and Friess, 2015; Levin et al., 2017; Walden-Schreiner et al., 2018).

Moreover in different counties, firewalls prevent some citizens from using different platforms. This can be overcome to some extent – Walden-Schreiner et al. (2018) used the machine learning algorithm MaxEnt, that *"assumes that data coverage is incomplete and provides predicted probabilities of presence based on combinations of factors"* (Walden-Schreiner et al., 2018: 785).

A further limitation relates to ethics and consent. Assessing the ethical issues and the ethical nature – or otherwise – of this research is fraught with difficulty and could be regarded as a moving feast. Kozinets (2019: 188) writes that:

> *Online research works with the massive amounts of personal data that are inadvertently and often without their producers' volition or permission being created by people's interactions with various online platforms, using their cell phones, laptops, desktops, tablets, set-top boxes, wearables, and other computing devices.*

Importantly, the practice of obtaining consent does not occur with online research, as it is often the case that participants are not contacted by the research team (Kozinets, 2019). Herein lies one of the major differences between research that uses data of this form and more traditional forms of research.

Many of the issues related to this method centre around recruitment, consent and privacy and the user agreements of the apps that are being used. Consequently, before research of this kind is undertaken, researchers must:

1. Review the terms and conditions of the social media site they plan to use;
2. Determine the legalities of their research in relation to their country and region where they are located;
3. Assesses the ethical requirements of their institution;
4. Assess the nature of posts they wish to assess to determine whether the posts were made to be viewed by the general public;
5. Ensure privacy is respected.

These five aspects will now be reviewed.

Instagram and **Facebook** have the same terms and conditions with regards to accessing their data:

"We prohibit crawling, scraping, caching or otherwise accessing any content on the Service via automated means, including but not limited to, user profiles and photos (except as may be the result of standard search engine protocols or technologies used by a search engine with Instagram's express consent)." (Instagram, 2017 General Conditions, Part 8)

Snapchat, with an estimated 186 million users in 2019, forbids the use of automation to access its data. This was reinforced by their actions in early 2019 when they introduced end-to end encryption embedded into its function so that photographs disappear. This is used by an estimated 16 million per day in the UK alone (The Telegraph, 2019).

At the time of writing, **Twitter** did not allow automated data scraping, but did offer three tiers of APIs in order to provide data. The most standard, free version allows sampling of tweets from the past 7 data. The 'premium' API offers both free and paid access to Tweets from the last 30 days or back to 2006. The third, 'enterprise' version, allows for paid access to historical data (Twitter, 2020).

For **Trip Advisor**, at the time of writing, the automated scaping without permission was also prohibited. An API is available for licenced partners. It states that "you agree not to …(ii) access, monitor, reproduce, distribute, transmit, broadcast, display, sell, license, copy or otherwise exploit any Content of the Services, including but not limited to, user profiles and photos, using any robot, spider, scraper or other automated means or any manual process for any purpose not in accordance with this Agreement or without our express written permission" (Trip Advisor, 2020).

WeChat's Acceptable Use Policy also prohibits the automated scraping of data. It states that:

"You agree not to engage in any of the following prohibited activities on or in relation to WeChat, or allow any person to use your account with us to do the same: …access any of WeChat, collect or process any content made available through WeChat, send or redirect any communications through WeChat, in each case, through the use of any automated bots, software, engines, crawlers, scrapers, data mining tools or the like, or attempt to do any of the foregoing" (WeChat, 2020).

Figure 5.4: Terms and Conditions of Facebook, Instagram, Snapchat, Twitter, Trip Advisor and WeChat.

Terms and Conditions

The End User License Agreements of many social media platforms outline how data from their platforms may be used. Social media platforms vary in their terms and conditions, but an overriding trend appears to be a tightening of the allowance of automated data scraping scripts such as those written in Python, or the use of bots as means to collate data (see Figure 5.4).

For example, this process is now banned for Facebook, Snapchat, Trip advisor and Instagram. As an alternative, some offer an API (at varying costs), which is a set of procedures that allow access to the data on the platform. If this is not able to be accessed, researchers have one further option – manual cut and paste procedures to allow data to be scraped. However great caution must be taken with this method, to ensure only public posts are used (detailed in the following paragraphs).

Legalities of research in researchers' country and region

Some jurisdictions operate under rules that may potentially allow the collation of scraped material from social media sites. For example, in the United States, the Fair Use rules potentially allow researchers to scrape data, under the Copyright Law of the United States (Title 17): (https://www.copyright.gov/title17/92chap1.html#107)

"Notwithstanding the provisions of sections 106 and 106A, the fair use of a copyrighted work, including such use by reproduction in copies or phonorecords or by any other means specified by that section, for purposes such as criticism, comment, news reporting, teaching (including multiple copies for classroom use), scholarship, or research, is not an infringement of copyright. In determining whether the use made of a work in any particular case is a fair use the factors to be considered shall include –

(1) the purpose and character of the use, including whether such use is of a commercial nature or is for nonprofit educational purposes;

(2) the nature of the copyrighted work;

(3) the amount and substantiality of the portion used in relation to the copyrighted work as a whole; and

(4) the effect of the use upon the potential market for or value of the copyrighted work.

The fact that a work is unpublished shall not itself bar a finding of fair use if such finding is made upon consideration of all the above factors."

Kozinets (2019) argues that despite these rules (a similar rule called 'fair dealing' exists in the UK), the GDPR is regarded as the default standard for research ethics. Research is said to occupy a privileged position within the GDPR – this issue was discussed in detail in Chapter 2, where it was highlighted that data privacy is a rapidly changing landscape and researchers must review the legal rules of their country and region before embarking on research of this nature.

Ethical requirements of researchers' institution

As was also mentioned in Chapter 2, researchers must abide by the ethical requirements of the institution within which they are working, as well as the ethical requirement that employees and the institution itself must abide by. In Australia as an example, the *National Statement on the Ethical Conduct of Research* (Commonwealth of Australia, 2018) was updated specifically to deal with social media research and particularly data scraping. Within this statement, consent occurs in three forms:

1. **Specific** – where participants give their consent to have their data used in a particular study;

2. **Extended** – where participants give their consent to have their data used in a particular study and in future studies that are closely related to it; and

3. **Unspecified** – where participants give their consent to have their data used in any future research.

The use of data from social media sites is problematic. Many social media platforms note in the Terms and Conditions that individual's data will be shared with other providers. Thus, it could be argued that the use of data that has been sourced via an API provided by the social media company is ethical, as users agree to the terms and conditions prior to being granted access to the social media platform. Conversely, it could be argued that individuals have not read the Terms and Conditions of the social media platform in detail, and may not realise their data could be shared by the company. This is particularly relevant for those with low literacy levels.

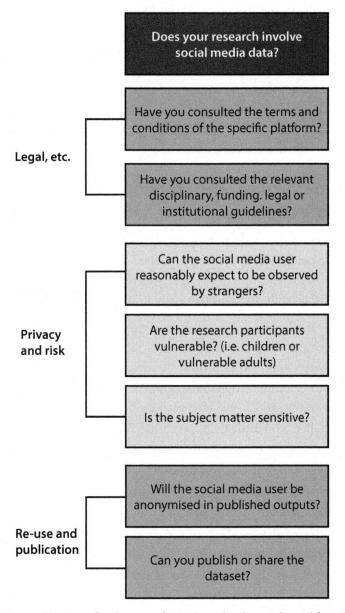

Figure 5.5: Decision making tree for the use of social media data. Adapted from Townsend and Wallace (2016: 197).

Given that data scraping (automated scraping, or via manual means) does not involve a process whereby consent is given, conservative approaches to the ethical conduct of research would argue, that because of this uncertainty around consent, it should not be used. However this approach is unusual – the common approach in Australia and the UK is illustrated in Figure 5.5 and suggests that if a post is public, legally sourced according to the end user agreement, not of a sensitive mature, does not reveal individuals' identity, and there were obvious attempts by the individual to increase the exposure of their posts (in the form of # and @), then efforts to conduct ethical research have been taken. The adapted table in Figure 5.5 was originally developed by Townsend and Wallace (2016) and is used as a guide in many universities in Australia and the United Kingdom.

Assessing posts to ensure intention to be viewed by the general public

User generated content often uses large amounts of data from participants who are not approached personally and asked to take part in studies. This is one of the most pressing issues related to how the data will be collected and therefore how ethical the research process will be.

If a small (and possibly private online group) is the unit of analysis, researchers will need to state what the study is about, gain permission from group, explain how the data will be collected, stored, analysed and where it will be used, give group members the opportunity to opt in to the study, and also give them access to their data, along with the chance to withdraw at any time without duress or consequence. This was the approach taken by Hardy and Dolnicar (2018) in their study of a Facebook group for Airbnb Hosts.

When researchers seek to gather data from large numbers of individuals who have posted, either via automated or non-automated collation of data, ethical collection of data must prevail. Researchers must ensure that the posts they assess were intended to be consumed by the general public – this becomes complicated when participants are not approached individually. On face value, it could be argued that the use of 'public' posts on social media have no ethical considerations, as the user has set up their profile so that it can be viewed and interpreted by the public. However, Kozinets (2019: 195) argues that:

'... *a significant number of people – very likely a majority – would prefer that researchers should not use their social media data and information in their investigations.*'

For example, it could be argued that not everyone has a high level of computer literacy, therefore they may not understand that their post is public; it is not uncommon that users unwittingly set their posts to 'public'.

It could be argued, as mentioned previously, that the use of symbols such as @ and # are attempts that further legitimise the use of social media posts, as they are attempts by individuals to increase their posts' exposure. This technique can be regarded as implied social media 'literacy'. However it should be used with caution; not all uses of @ or # are attempts to be public – some social media users use hashtags to create private catalogues of their images for their use private use only.

Finally, the person who sets the account up may not be an adult – in Australia, research involving children triggers a requirement for a higher level of ethical approval from the child and/or their guardian.

Consequently, Kozinets (2019: 187) expresses concern over what he refers to as being the consent gap:

'*In written and presented work that uses social media data, academics often insist that, when people post things on public facing web applications like Instagram or Twitter, they already know that what they are posting is public.*'

Consequently Kozinets (2019) recommends that researchers should use opportunities to gain permission and consent whenever possible.

It is also worth noting that while public posts may be included in studies, users may change their settings and delete posts. There is a risk that if users change their posts after the data collection phase has been conducted, their post will be included in the analysis despite no longer meeting the criteria in its present form. In the absence of gaining consent from those who have posted, the only option for mitigating this risk is that researchers should double check the posts they report on (e.g. when using quotes in reporting) immediately before their work is published, to ensure that they are still publicly available.

Ensuring privacy

A further consideration of the use of data from social media accounts pertains to imagery. There is the potential for the identity and location of users to be revealed through photos and text that contain identifying information. This is particularly important if data is to be collated in close to, or actual, real time. Consequently, researchers must go to great efforts to ensure that users' data is not potentially identifiable (Girardin et al. 2008). This may be done through anonymising, using pseudonyms and deleting identifying location information, plus delaying reporting beyond real time.

While methods have been developed to differentiate tourists from locals, this differentiation is based on a formula and anomalies may occur. While this method produces vast amount of data, the real identify of users is not always able to be gained from post content, therefore data on how tourists travel must be viewed with caution.

Platform and user bias

A further issue relates to the use of different social media platforms. Social media platforms wax and wane in their popularity and these changes can be rapid. While Foursquare was immensely popular five years ago, it could be argued that the Google Review function has led to its demise. Currently Snapchat, TikTok, WeChat and Instagram are immensely popular amongst young people, whereas Facebook was dominant several years ago. Each platform attracts a different demographic, and many choose to use different platforms at different times and for different friend or family groups. Moreover, many people now choose to make their posts private. While syncing data sets from different social media platforms may lessen this bias, Girardin et al. (2008) noted the difficulty in doing this. Wong, Law and Li (2017) also noted the limitations of using less popular platforms such as Panoramio and Flickr, as did Sobolevsky et al. (2015), who tracked tourists using both credit card and social media posts. They determined that in some places, such as Alicante, visitation was evident from tourists' credit card transactions, but they were less likely to post on social media about their visit to the destination. They also noted that some destinations did not match the demographic of certain social media users; in their case it was Twitter and Flickr. Finally, they noted that compulsive users may appear multiple times in the same location, and this, if not addressed, can muddle the data.

Non-continual data and reliance on geotagging

There are a variety of additional limitations with this method. The first is that it is a non-continual method. Researchers may only use the data that has been posted by the user at a certain point in time, and this may not reflect their actual behavioural patterns. For those users who manually geotag, there may also be issues related to the accuracy of tagging. Incorrect tagging of locations can occur (intentionally or otherwise) so cleaning and checking photographs or text is necessary (Garcia-Palomores, Gutierrez, and Minguez, 2015; Wong, Law and Li, 2017). It is also worth noting that confusion can occur when places have similar names (Mukhina, Rakitin and Vishertin, 2017). Related to this, if the time stamp on the camera is not correct, this can cause errors in understanding movement through time (Girardin et al., 2008) and more importantly, due to privacy concerns, not everyone uses the geo-location function (Mukhina, Rakitin and Vishertin, 2017).

Conclusion

The use of geotagged social media posts offer researchers the opportunity to access vast amounts of data that can be useful to assess crowding and infrastructure use. The ability to sync geotagged movement data with experimental data that can be sourced from users' comments, plus the vast amount of data and its low cost, makes it a very attractive option for researchers.

Importantly, this form of data is non-continuous. The precise itineraries of tourists cannot be gained from this data as it relies on posts that are geotagged, rather than continual tracking. Moreover, the tightening of Terms and Conditions of many social media platforms means that accessing this data is now a major issue. Automated scraping is now largely illegal, and APIs may be expensive. Manual scraping of data is time-consuming. There are significant ethical challenges, which, while not always insurmountable, must be taken into consideration by researchers who use this method. Future research that uses this form of data should proceed, albeit in an ethical and cautionary manner.

Key learnings from this chapter:

- Geo-tagged social media data is becoming increasingly difficult to obtain due to the tightening of applications' terms and conditions.

- Data from social media platforms may be obtained via scaping, an API (application programming interface) or via manual collection.

- Research using this method has resulted in insights into sequence of movement, crowding and popularity of sites in time and space.

- Geo-tagged social media data is limited in its ability to provide socio-demographic data or an understanding of the sequence of movement taken by tourists.

- The covert nature of this technique means that consent and privacy remain significant issues when using this form of data.

References

Chua, A., Servillo, L., Marcheggiani, E. and Vande Moere, A. (2016) Mapping Cilento: Using geotagged social media data to characterize tourist flows in Southern Italy. *Tourism Management*, **57**, 295-310

Chung, N and Lee, H. (2016) Sharing economy in geotag: what are the travelers' goals in sharing their locations by geotags in social network sites during the tour?, *International Journal of Tourism Cities*, **2**(2), 125-136.

Commonwealth of Australia (2018) *National Statement on Ethical Conduct in Human Research, .* The National Health and Medical Research Council, the Australian Research Council and Universities Australia.

Cristina, L. and Stoleriu, O.M (2020) Spatial patterns of tourists preferences in Romanian cities using TripAdvisor, In Stienmetz, Ferrer-Rosell & Schuckert (eds.) *Proceedings of the ENTER2020 Ph.D. Workshop*, Surrey, England.

Diamantini, C. Genga, L. Marozzo, F. Potena, D. and Trunfio, P. (2017) Discovering mobility patterns of instagram users through process mining techniques, In *Proceedings of the 2017 IEEE International Conference on Information Reuse and Integration* (IRI), San Diego, 485–492.

Dickinger, A., Scharl, A., Stern, H., Weichselbraun, A. and Wöber, K. (2008) Acquisition and relevance of geotagged information in tourism, In P. O'Connor., W. Hopken & U. Gretzel (Eds.), *Proceedings of Information and Communication Technologies in Tourism 2008*, Springer, 545–555.

Garcia-Palomores, J., Gutierrez,J. and Minguez, C. (2015) Identification of tourist hot spots based on social networks: A comparative analysis of European metropolises using photo-sharing services and GIS, *Applied Geography*, **63**, 408-417.

Girardin, F., Calabrese, F., Fiore, F.D., Ratti, C. and Blat, J. (2008) Digital footprinting: uncovering tourists with user-generated content, *Pervasive Computing*, **7**(4), 36-43.

Gavric, K.D., Culibrk, D.R., Lugonja, P.I., Mirkovic, M.R. and Crnojevic, V.S. (2011) Detecting attractive locations and tourists' dynamics using geo-referenced images. 10th International Conference on Telecommunication in Modern Satellite Cable and Broadcasting Services (TELSIKS), 208-211, Belgrade, Oct 5–8.

Gikas, J. and Grant, M. (2013) Mobile computing devices in higher education: student perspectives on learning with cellphones, smartphones and social media, *The Internet and Higher Education*, **19**, 18-26.

Gou, S., Li, G., Zhang, K., Liang, Y. and Zhou, J. (2016) Space-time behaviour of "tourists" based on self-media platform: A case study of Professor W's WeChat moments, *Tourism Tribune*, **31**(8), 71–80.

Gretzel, U. and Hardy, A., (2019) # VanLife: Materiality, makeovers and mobility amongst digital nomads. *E-review of Tourism Research*, 16(2/3), 1-9.

Guo, L., Li, Z., and Sun, W. (2015). Understanding travel destination from structured tourism blogs. In *Proceedings of 2015 Wuhan International Conference on e-Business* (pp. 144–151).

5

Hardy, A. and Dolnicar, S. (2018) Networks and hosts: a love-hate relationship, In S Dolnicar (ed) *Peer-to-Peer Accommodation Networks: Pushing the boundaries*, Goodfellow Publishers, Oxford, pp. 182-194.

Hausmann, A., T. Toivonen, R. Slotow, H. Tenkanen, A. Moilanen, V. Heikinheimo and E. Di Minin. (2017) Social media data can be used to understand tourists' preferences for nature-based experiences in protected areas, *Conservation Letters*, **11**(1), 1-10.

Hawelka, B., Sitko, I., Beinat, E., Sobolevsky, S., Kazakopoulos, P. and Ratti, C. (2014) Geo-located Twitter as proxy for global mobility patterns, *Cartography and Geographic Information Science*, **41**, 260-271.

Instagram (2017) Terms of Use, Available from https://help.instagram.com/1188470931252371 [Accessed 27th August 2019]

Jiang, K., Wang, P. and Yu, N. (2011) ContextRank: Personalized tourism recommendation by exploiting context information of geotagged web photos, in *Proceedings of IEEE16th International Conference on Image and Graphics*, 931–937.

Kachkaev, A. and Wood, J. (2013). Investigating spatial patterns in user-generated photographic datasets by means of interactive visual analytics. Paper presented at the GeoViz Hamburg: Interactive Maps that Help People Think, 6–8 Mar, HafenCity University, Hamburg, Germany

Kádár, B. (2014) Measuring tourist activities in cities using geotagged photography, *Tourism Geographies*, **16** (1), 88-104.

Kádár, B. and Gede, M. (2013) Where do tourists go? Visualizing and analysing the spatial distribution of geotagged photography, *Cartographica*, **48**(2),78–88.

Kisilevich, S., Keim, D., Andrienko, N., Andrienko, G. (2013) Towards acquisition of semantics of places and events by multi-perspective analysis of geotagged photo collections, in A. Moore and I. Drecki (Eds.), *Geospatial Visualisation, Lecture Notes in Geoinformation and Cartography*, Springer-Verlag, Berlin Heidelberg

Koerbitz, W., Önder, I. and Hubmann-Haidvogel, A.C. (2013) Identifying tourist dispersion in Austria by digital footprints, in L. Cantoni, Z. Xiang (Eds.), *Information and Communication Technologies in Tourism 2013*, Springer Verlag Berlin Heidelberg, 495-506.

Kozinets, R. (2019) *Netnography: The Essential Guide to Qualitative Social Media Research*. Third Edition, SAGE Publications.

Levin, N., Lechner, A.M. and Brown, G. (2017) An evaluation of crowdsourced information for assessing the visitation and perceived importance of protected areas, *Applied Geography*, **79**, 115–126.

Levin, N., Kark, S. and Crandall, D. (2015) Where have all the people gone? Enhancing global conservation using night lights and social media, *Ecological Applications*, **25**, 2153–2167.

Mukhina, K.D., Rakitin, S. and Vishertin, A. (2017) Detection of tourists attraction points using Instagram profiles, in *Proceedings of the International Conference on Computational Science*, Zurich Switzerland, 2378-2382.

Popescu, A., Grefenstette, G. and Moëllic, P.A. (2009) Mining tourist information from user-supplied collections, Paper presented at the Conference on Information and Knowledge Management, http://comupedia.org/adrian/articles/sp0668-popescu.pdf [Accessed 6th May 2020]

Ramasco, J. J. (2016) Touristic site attractiveness seen through Twitter, *EPJ Data Science*, **5**(1), 12.

Richards, D.R. and D.A. Friess (2015) A rapid indicator of cultural ecosystem service usage at a fine spatial scale: Content analysis of social media photographs, *Ecological Indicators*, **53**, 187–195.

Rossi, L.; Boscaro, E.; Torsello, A. (2018) Venice through the lens of Instagram: A visual narrative of tourism in Venice. In *Proceedings of the Companion of the Web Conference*, Lyon, France, 1190–1197.

Salas-Olmedo, M.H., Moya-Gómez, B., García-Palomares, J.C. and Gutiérrez, J. (2018) Tourists' digital footprint in cities: Comparing Big Data sources, *Tourism Management*, **66**, 13-25.

See, L., P. Mooney, G. Foody, L. Bastin, A. Comber, J. Estima, S. Fritz, N. Kerle et al. (2016) Crowdsourcing, citizen science or volunteered geographic information? The current state of crowdsourced geographic information, *International Journal of Geo-Information*, **5** (5), 55.

Sobolevsky, S., Bojic, I., Belyi, A., Sitko, I., Hawelka, B. and Arias, J. M.(2015) Scaling of city attractiveness for foreign visitors through big data of human economical and social media activity, in Big data (BigData Congress), 2015 IEEE International Congress, 600-607.

Sonter, L.J., Watson, K.B., Wood, S.A. and Ricketts, T.H. (2016) Spatial and temporal dynamics and value of nature-based recreation, estimated via social media, *PLoS One*, **11**(9), doi:10.1371/ journal.pone.0162372 0162372.

5

Spalding, M., Burke, L., Wood, S.A., Ashpole, J., Hutchison, J. and Ermgassen, P. (2017) Mapping the global value and distribution of coral reef tourism, *Marine Policy*, **82**, 104–113.

Straumann, R.K., Çöltekin, A. and Andrienko, G. (2014) Towards (re) constructing narratives from georeferenced photographs through visual analytics', *The Cartographic Journal*, **51**(2), 152-165.

Tammet, T., Luberg, A. and Järv, P. (2013). Sightsmap: crowd-sourced popularity of the world places. In *Information and Communication Technologies in Tourism 2013*. Springer Verlag, Berlin, Heidelberg, pp. 314-325.

Tenkanen, T., Di Minin, E. Heikinheimo, V., Hausmann,A., Her, M., Kajala, L. and Toivonen. T. (2017) Instagram, Flickr, or Twitter: Assessing the usability of social media data for visitor monitoring in protected areas, *Scientific Reports*, **7**(1), 1-11.

The Telegraph (2019) Snapchat adds end-to-end encryption to protect users' messages, https://www.telegraph.co.uk/technology/2019/01/09/snapchat-adds-end-to-end-encryption-protect-users-messages/ [Accessed 27th August 2019]

Townsend, L. and Wallace, C. (2016) Social media research: A guide to ethics, Working paper published by the University of Aberdeen https://www.gla.ac.uk/media/Media_487729_smxx.pdf. [Accessed 4th February 2020]

Trip Advisor (2020) Media Centre. Available from https://tripadvisor.mediaroom.com/ie-terms-of-use [Accessed 5th August 2020]

Twitter, (2020)Twitter terms of service. Available from https://twitter.com/en/tos [Accessed 5th August 2020]

van der Zee, E., Bertocchi, D. and Vanneste, D. (2020) Distribution of tourists within urban heritage destinations: a hot spot/cold spot analysis of TripAdvisor data as support for destination management, *Current Issues in Tourism*, **23**(2), 175-196.

Vu, H., Li, G, Law, R. and Ye, B. (2015) Exploring the travel behaviors of inbound tourists to Hong Kong using geotagged photos, *Tourism Management*, **46**, 222-232.

Walden-Schreiner, C., Dario Rossi, S., Barros, A. Pickering, C. and Leung, Y. (2018) Using crowd-sourced photos to assess seasonal patterns of visitor use in mountain-protected areas, *Ambio*, **47**, 781–793.

WeChat. (2020) Acceptable Use Policy. [Available from https://www.wechat. com/en/acceptable_use_policy.html [Accessed 26th March 2020]

Wong, E., Law R., Li G. (2017) Reviewing geotagging research in tourism. In: Schegg R., Stangl B. (eds) *Information and Communication Technologies in Tourism 2017*. Springer, Cham.

Xiang, Z. and Gretzel, U., (2010) Role of social media in online travel information search. *Tourism Management*, **31** (2), 179-188.

Yoo, K. H. and Gretzel, U. (2010). Antecedents and impacts of trust in travel-related consumer-generated media. *Information Technology & Tourism*, **12**(2), 139-152.

Zheng, Y. T., Zha, Z. J. and Chua, T. S. (2012) Mining travel patterns from geotagged photos, *Transactions on Intelligent Systems and Technology*, **3**(3), 56–73.

Zhou, B., Liu, L., Oliva, A. and Torralba, A. (2014). Recognizing city identity via attribute analysis of geotagged images. In Fleet , D., Pajdla, T., Schiele, B., Tuytelaars, T. (Eds), *European Conference on Computer Vision–ECCV 2014 Proceedings*, Springer International Publishing, 519-534.

5

6 Tracking via Volunteered Geographic Information

What this chapter will cover:

- How mHealth apps can be used to produce continuous location-based data, or volunteered geographic information (VGI), for researchers.

- The contributions that VGI has made to understanding tourist and recreationalists mobility within urban and non-urban parks.

- The possibility to use this data as a proxy for visitation in some urban settings.

- The limitations of this form of data in terms of accessing data, its limited socio-demographic capabilities and the need to ensure ethical research procedures.

Introduction

Over the past 20 years, the use of location-based tracking has become increasingly popular. The introduction of GPS technology into devices such as phones and watches, and its incorporation into tracking apps, has led to widespread use of apps which track activities, particularly those of a sporting nature. There are now over 318,000 health and fitness apps – called mHealth apps (Byambasuren et al., 2018) – and it is estimated that 75% of runners now use them (Janssen et al., 2017). Many of these apps contain the ability for users to track their movement and share it with fellow app users – Strava alone has 42 million accounts with 1 million users each month (Haden, 2019), but others include MapMyFitness, Adidas Running, and Google Fit.

Importantly for this book, the data that is produced from mHealth apps is continuous point geo-referenced data that is visualised for the user as a defined route undertaken during a particular activity. This route, and the temporal and spatial aspects of the activity, can be viewed by the user and then released online for their online network to view. Most commonly, it is referred to as volunteered geographic information (VGI). The data that is generated from mHealth apps can be sourced by researchers; this is often referred to as crowd sourcing. Researchers can gather large amounts of data of entire paths taken by individual users, either via gaining consent from individual users to share their routes, or via APIs provided by the app developer which provide access to large amounts of routes and their associated statistics.

VGI provides researchers with great potential to facilitate research that assesses tourists' movement through space and time (Heikinheimo et al., 2017). However, as is the case with single point geo-referenced data (discussed in the previous chapter), research in this space is disparate and tends to focus on one platform at a time, or one context at a time.

The rapid increase in VGI is arguably due to three factors: developments in wearable technology; developments in location based technology that has been integrated into smart phone and watch apps; and an increase in usage of urban spaces for walking, running and biking. The latter is largely due to an increased interest in healthy lifestyles and exercise (Santos et al., 2016; Brown et al., 2014) and presents issues for park managers, including those related to environmental impacts due to overuse and conflicts between different types of users, such as walkers and bike riders (Santos et al., 2016; Norman and Pickering, 2017; Pickering et al., 2011; Rossi et al., 2013). This chapter will explore how VGI data can assist researchers and managers in understanding these issues, along with tourists' mobility.

How mHealth apps work

mHealth applications (apps) are designed to track individuals' speed, distance, elevation, time, plus physiological factors such as heartrate and energy expenditure, when doing exercise. The apps can be placed on individuals' smart phones or watches and then downloaded so that users can view their statistics, along with their networks, should they wish to share their data.

Many companies who have developed these apps make their money from selling the aggregated data of their app users.

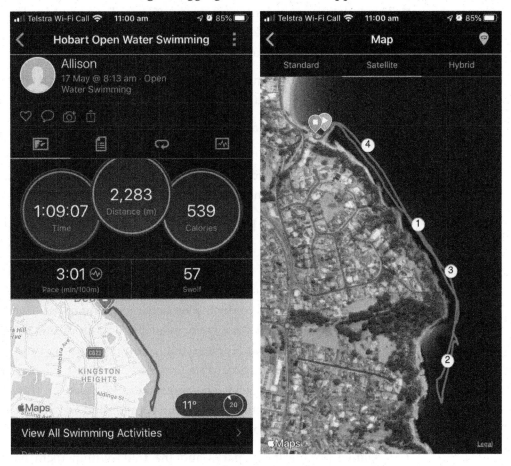

Figure 6.1: Example screen shot of mHealth app Garmin ConnectTM

What has been explored using this method

Contributions to our understanding of mobility via VGI have largely been in the recreational space in relation to park usage, including urban parks and national parks. Work in this area has led to understandings of mobility and tourism/leisure in a number of areas, which will be explored in the following section. They include:

- The relative popularity of different parks (Norman, Pickering and Castley, 2019; Norman and Pickering, 2017);

- The relative popularity of trails (Campelo and Mendes, 2016; Norman and Pickering, 2017; Norman et al., 2019; Korplio, Virtanen and Lehavirta, 2017);

- Areas of potential conflict between different recreational user groups (Santos et al., 2016);

- Off-trail use (Norman and Pickering, 2017);

- Comparative usage patterns of different recreational user groups – e.g. mountain bike riders, runners and walkers (Norman et al., 2019; Korplio, Virtanen and Lehavirta, 2017);

- Factors contributing to parks' popularity (Norman and Pickering, 2019).

In an early application of this form of tracking, Santos et al. (2016) assessed the spatial overlap of different user groups in order to determine where the potential for conflicts may occur in urban parks. They sourced 2,769,363 tracks that were freely available data from trail app GPSies, and assessed the spatial interaction of different users (tracks are classified by GPSies users according to their activity, e.g. running, hiking, biking, horse riding, etc). The researchers focussed on 'high use' tracks used by both mountain bikers and runners and were able to identify trails where there was a high potential for conflict.

The relative popularity of parks and the trails within them has been explored by Norman, Pickering and Castley (2019). They used VGI from MapMyFitness to compare how mountain bikers, runners and walkers used different reserves in Brisbane, Australia. They found that mountain biking was the most popular activity and that the route data from MapMyFitness was very effective at predicting the relative popularity of different trails. They concluded that this form of data can be very useful for planners and managers as it illustrates use of parks by different types of recreational users (e.g. mountain bikers vs runners vs walkers), plus entry into non-authorised areas such as adjacent private land. Their study confirmed previous research that has suggested apps such as MapMyFitness can be used as an accurate proxy for understanding patterns of use on popular trails (see the later section on Advantages for a detailed discussion of this point).

Trail usage has also been explored by Korpilo, Virtanen and Lehavirta (2017). These authors assessed trail popularity through their analysis of the spatial distribution and density of 55 runners and mountain bikers in an urban forest in Central Park, Helsinki. They used a different method to obtain Strava and Sports Tracker app data. First the researchers recruited volunteers face to face and asked them to share their data with the research team via email. Second the research team recruited participants online and asked them to share their data via email. Both recruitment techniques de-identified all the data that they used to ensure confidentiality and anonymity, while personal recruitment ensured that informed consent underpinned the study. Given that participants had different mobile phones and used different apps, the research team had to conduct a visual analysis to determine whether the data deviated from the GPS tracks of the formal trail network. Differences were found, so proximity analysis was conducted, and they generated a 'near table' tool to aggregate and account for the deviations. Their research found that mountain bikers tended to leave trails more frequently – these were able to be mapped as 'hotspots' of off-trail usage.

Rice et al. (2019) also used Strava to develop visitor insights for park managers. They overlayed existing trail network maps with data from Strava heat maps function (where users can view an area virtually to get a sense of its use and location). Norman et al. (2019) also conducted research to assist park managers. They demonstrated that in the short term, apps such as MapMyFitness can provide information on resource conflict – they found that the greatest risk was on a Sunday when trails close to the entry of the parks were popular amongst both mountain bikers and walkers.

6

Finally, Norman and Pickering (2019) were able to demonstrate the effects of distance decay, in terms of parks' proximity from urban centres. They also determined predictive factors that appear to make parks popular – e.g. for adventure-focused Wikiloc users, the elevation of a park was found to be a good predictor of its popularity, whereas proximity to urban centres was a good predictor of park popularity for more fitness-focused Strava and MapMyFitness users.

Methodological explorations of VGI data

In additional to conceptual understandings that have emerged from the use of VGI data, there is a growing body of research that explored the methodology and made findings that will assist future users of this data. Many of these findings relate to the comparative efficacy of the great range of mHealth apps that are available for researchers.

Early research in this space suggested that great variation in accuracy occurred across mHealth apps. In 2013, Bauer (2013) found significant differences. The author downloaded nine sporting applications on the same smartphone and assessed their distance accuracy. She found some apps were up to 60 metres inaccurate when used on a runner who ran 1000 metres. The author also found that some of the applications visualised a zigzagging track, despite the test person running in a straight line. Similar variations were found when altitude, ascents, and descents were tested.

However, in later research, Campelo and Mendes (2016) found similar results between apps. Their research compared GPSies and Wikloc to study mountain bike users. They assessed the tracks that were generated from both apps in the Portuguese Sintra-Cascais Natural Park and determined that different apps performed in quite a similar fashion. More recently, Conrow et al. (2018) explored the correlation between crowd sourced data from Strava and conventional forms of data. They conducted their study in Greater Sydney, obtaining the data from Strava metro (the commercial data product produced by Strava for planners, advocacy groups and researchers) which aggregates data in order to protect users' identity. They compared this with a manual count of cyclists that was conducted during the peak commuting time of 7am-9am in 2016 in eight locations across 12 council areas in Greater Sydney. Their research revealed differences between the manual count and the Strava dataset – they found higher ridership levels amongst Strava users in the eastern suburbs of Sydney which are not high employment centres – riders there were more likely to be riding for fitness and competition, rather than commuters. But, in the central business district, there was a strong correlation between Strava users and the conventional count in terms of where areas of ridership concentration occurred. They concluded that VGI/crowd sourced data can be useful for planners to design and plan cycling facilities and argued that Strava offers much more detailed data than manual counting as it has both spatial and temporal abilities. Their study was also able to determine areas where ridership levels were low – in their case they found low ridership levels in areas with a lower socio-economic status and areas with lower percentages of residential land use. Their study built upon previous research – such as the work of Heesch and Langdon (2017) – that used this form of data to demonstrate how changes in infrastructure affects behaviour.

6

Apps have also been compared in terms of their usage and ability to assess behaviour. In Queensland, Australia, Norman and Pickering (2017) compared three apps (MapMyFitness, Wikiloc and GPSies) to assess different types of park visitation: peri-urban, urban and a remote park. The parks were commonly used for walking and running. The research team found clear differences in usage data from the three apps, aside from their popularity (MapMyFitness was the most popular at the time of their study). They found the users of apps differed in their behaviour; they found that those using MapMyFitness tended not to leave formal trails, and greater evidence of use of informal trails in more remote parks on Wikiloc.

In a more recent study, Norman and Pickering (2019) compared MapMyFitness, Strava and Wikiloc to assess the relative popularity of 40 national parks in Southeast Queensland, Australia. They found that Strava and MapMyFitness showed similar trends in terms of park popularity and route usage. However, they were very different to Wikiloc which was more frequently used by those in more remote parks who undertook off-trail walks.

In light of this, Norman and Pickering (2017) recommended complementing data from these apps with other data sources such as trail counters and direct observation for a comprehensive understanding of parks usage. Counts are limited on their own as they do not tell researchers where people actually go, while apps are good for understanding relative use of different trails.

Advantages of using VGI data

There are many advantages to using data from VGI mHealth apps. They can provide vast amounts of detail on the spatial and temporal mobility patterns of users (Campelo and Mendes, 2016; Santos et al., 2016). Most importantly, unlike many other forms of tracking data, a continuous track can be gained, so great detail can be gained into the precise movement patterns of individuals. This method is very good for shorter trips and non-motorised activities because it provides fine grained data, which is what needed to really understand mobility at this scale (Cervero and Duncan, 2003).

mHealth apps also provide very large data sets at very low cost (Foody et al., 2014; Korplio, Virtanen and Lehavirta, 2017). The method of research is also very user-friendly as participants can use their own phones or watches and don't need to carry a device, or download a study-specific app. This also reduces the cost and risk of equipment being lost (Korplio, Virtanen and Lehavirta, 2017) while offering a low resource method of data collection (Campelo and Mendes, 2016).

mHealth apps are also particularly good for understanding spatial patterns of use, including errant behaviour, such as was the case with the Korpilo et al. study (2017) that revealed those more likely to engage in off-trail behaviour. They argued that this method is also very useful for collecting timely data; trail use can often change quickly if new trails are created from off-trail use, and this method can promptly identify this occurring.

The data that emerges from mHealth apps, particularly in urban areas, has recently been determined as being appropriate as a proxy for more traditional forms of tracking such as head counts and trail counters. A variety of researchers, using data from Strava and MapMyFitness, have demonstrated correlations in the relative popularity of destinations and trails, between volunteered geographic information and on-site data (Norman et al., 2019; Heikinheimo et al., 2017; Conrow et al., 2018).

Limitations of using VGI data

Like all tracking methods, the use of data generated from VGI/mHealth apps does have limitations. Relying on this data alone will have an inherent bias to those who use mHealth apps. It should be remembered that different types of users are attracted to different app style and this should be taken into account when considering user bias (Campelo and Mendes, 2016; Salas-Olmedo, 2018; Conrow et al., 2018). Conrow et al. (2018) suggested that reliance on mHealth apps can overlook children, commuters, students and average recreational riders, for example. Norman and Pickering (2017) noted that MapMyFitness is used by those wishing to track their fitness and to share information on their routes and times. Conversely, GPSies and Wikiloc are more commonly used by people in remote areas who wish to share their GPS routes with their online connections. The same authors also noted that different apps come in and out of fashion, so that longitudinal studies that rely on single apps may not necessarily be good proxies for usage.

Usage of different apps across different areas is also an issue; Heesch and Langdon (2017) found that while mHealth location data was good to understand how new infrastructure changed behaviour, conventional data was needed as there were variations in how different apps were used across their study area.

There are also issues related to technology. If existing applications on individual mobile devices such as watches and mobile phones are used (e.g. Strava) then researchers must take into account the mobile phone device, its operating system and also the functionality of the tracking application, as these can influence the quality of the GPS accuracy (Korpil, Virtanen and Lehavirta, 2017).

6

Furthermore, there are also issues related to participants interaction with the apps. Norman and Pickering (2017) note there can be reluctance to use tracking devices such as GPS devices. There is also the possibility that the knowledge that someone is being tracked may affect their behaviour (Newsome et al., 2012), but the impact of this phenomena is largely unknown in this field. Similarly, this form of data, unless combined with survey, is unable to determine users' motivations. Moreover, there are also privacy issues – home locations may be revealed with this method. There are also issues related to illegal behaviour while using apps (Oksanen et al., (2015). The requirement to overlook or report illegal behaviour depends upon the institution and country where research is being conducted and researchers are advised to investigate this option with their research institution or relevant ethics committee.

Increasingly, one of the challenges to using mHealth apps relates to the accessibility of data. This is changing constantly; Strava now requires payment to access usage data; whereas GPSies provides an API that allows researchers to access publicly available data. And finally, Norman and Pickering (2017) found that the forest canopy did cause some issues in determining precise routes taken by those using the apps. The reliance of mHealth apps on access to satellites in order to determine their location means that their use is restricted to outdoor environments and can be subject to multipath errors in highly urbanised or forested areas.

And finally, while there is strong evidence of an increase in use of mHealth apps by researchers wishing to understand mobility of recreational cyclists, hikers and runners within urban areas, urban parks, peri-urban parks and non-urban parks, the use of mHealth apps to collate data on *tourism* is almost non-existent. There is great potential to change this; mHealth apps can provide large amounts of detail on behaviour and are relatively unobtrusive given their ability to be used on participants' own devices. However, what is yet to be known is the level of resistance to this kind of research, and the length of time that participants would be willing to engage in it.

Ethical considerations

As with social media apps, the availability of location-based data for researchers is constantly evolving and researchers should pay strict attention to each apps' Terms of Use. At the time of writing, Strava did not allow the use of web scraping and web harvesting. Researchers are required to engage with its commercial arm, Strava Metro, who has developed a dashboard for visualisations of the data, along with CSV files of the raw data (Strava, 2020). In some instances, the data is provided free of charge, but the platform has largely been designed to make money from the sale of data.

As with the use of social media data, one of the ethical issues that faces researchers who source large amounts of data via an API or scraping, is whether app users were explicitly aware of how their data would be used. The Terms and Conditions for end users state that data will be used, but whether or not users of the applications understand that their data may be on-sold or shared with researchers, requires further investigation.

6

While apps have Terms and Conditions that are required by law to clearly state where individuals' data goes, some researchers have chosen non-automated methods to collate users' data and ensure informed consent. Korpilo, Virtanen and Lehvarvirta (2017), approached Strava users in a park in Helsinki and online, and asked them if the researchers could become connected to the potential participants via the app, so that they could view their movement. This approach ensured that would-be participants could be made aware of what the study involved; could opt-in rather than opt out; and ensured participants were made aware of how their data would be used, how it would be stored and for how long the data would be used for and by whom; and that their participation would be anonymous and confidential; plus they were offered the opportunity to be given feedback on the results of the study.

Finally, as with all tracking data, researchers must ensure the privacy of the individual by ensuring that their home location, work location, and identity is not revealed. This is particularly important if real time, or close-to-real-time data is being used.

Conclusion

The rapid growth in popularity of mHealth apps that collect very fine grained data (often referred to as volunteer generated information) on individuals' spatial and temporal movement offers many opportunities for researchers to collate data that can often be regarded as a proxy for actual visitation patterns, in a timely and cost efficient manner. While mHealth app usage is not ubiquitous and therefore cannot be considered as a substitute for actual visitation numbers, the data they produce on behavioural patterns can produce tangible and often very reliable insights for park managers and planners, who wish to plan new infrastructure, or assess the impact of it. It is also a very useful data source for understanding the potential for resource conflict, particularly when multiple user groups use the same areas. The data has also been found to be a very useful tool for understanding errant behaviour, such as off track walking or illegal access.

This form of data does have limitations. Its application to recreation research is now common, but it has rarely been used in tourism. This is because mHealth apps tend to be used by those who are recreating using sport, such as mountain bike riding or running. While tourists may appear in broader data sets on park usage, they are not generally the focus of this type of research and are difficult to identify as the geo-located data often contains little demographic information.

Part of the reason why the application of mHealth apps in tourism research may be limited could be due to its inability to provide more than geo-location data. It is difficult for researchers to determine which users are tourists, and the data that is created is often de-identified, so travel preferences, behaviour and motivations cannot be synced with geo-location data automatically via the app. The only means that this could be done would be if a survey was combined with individuals' data – and this can be a costly and logistically difficult solution.

Despite these limitations, the use of mHealth app data has led to significant findings in recreation research. The apps' popularity offers many opportunities for future tourism and leisure research.

Key learnings from this chapter:

- mHealth apps offer researchers the ability to access continuous location-based data, or volunteered geographic information (VGI).

- The high rates of use of these apps mean that data from these apps can often be used a proxies for rates of visitation.

- Data from this method has resulted in significant insights into how different user groups use urban and non-urban parks.

- This method is limited in that different apps attract different segments of the population and the apps are more widely used in urban settings.

- Researchers must ensure that individuals' home locations are not revealed when using this data and must also take steps to ensure data was accessed ethically.

- Volunteered geographic information is limited in its ability to collect socio-demographic and traveller preference data.

6

References

Bauer, C. (2013) On the (in)accuracy of GPS measures of smartphones: A study of running tracking applications, In *Proceedings of 11th Conference on Advances in Mobile Computing & Multimedia* (pp. 335-341).

Brown, G., Schebella, M.F. and Weber, D. (2014) Using participatory GIS to measure physical activity and urban park benefits, *Landscape and Urban Planning*, **121**, 34–44.

Byambasuren, O., Sanders, S., Beller, E. and Glasziou, P. (2018) Prescribable mHealth apps identified from an overview of systematic reviews, *NPJ Digital Medicine* **b**(1), 1-12.

Campelo, M. B. and Mendes, R. M. N. (2016) Comparing webshare services to assess mountain bike use in protected areas, *Journal of Outdoor Recreation and Tourism*, **15**, 82–88.

Cervero, R. and Duncan, M. (2003) Walking, bicycling, and urban landscapes: Evidence from the San Francisco Bay area, *American Journal of Public Health*, **93**(9), 1478–1483.

Conrow, L., Wentz, E., Nelson, T. and Pettit, C. (2018) Comparing spatial patterns of crowdsourced and conventional bicycling datasets, *Applied Geography*, **92**, 21-30.

Foody, G. M., See, L., Fritz, S., Van der Velde, M., Perger, C., Schill, C., Boyd, D.S. and Comber, A. (2015) Accurate attribute mapping from volunteered geographic information: issues of volunteer quantity and quality, *The Cartographic Journal*, **52** (4), 336-344.

Haden, J. (2019) Strava has 42 million users and adds 1 million more each month. Will it be the next great sports brand?' Inc., Available from: https://www.inc.com/jeff-haden/10-years-in-strava-now-adds-1-million-users-a-month-but-can-it-become-next-great-sports-brand.html [accessed 5th August 2020].

Heesch, K. C., and Langdon, M. (2017) The usefulness of GPS bicycle tracking data for evaluating the impact of infrastructure change on cycling behaviour, *Health Promotion Journal of Australia*, **27**(3), 222–229.

Heikinheimo, V., Minin, E. D., Tenkanen, H., Hausmann, A., Erkkonen, J. and Toivonen, T. (2017) User-generated geographic information for visitor monitoring in a national park: A comparison of social media data and visitor survey. ISPRS International, *Journal of Geo-Information*, **6**(3), 85.

Janssen, M., Scheerder, J., Thibaut, E., Brombacher, A. and Vos, S. (2017) Who uses running apps and sports watches? Determinants and consumer profiles of event runners ' usage of running-related smartphone applications and sports watches, *PloS one*, **12** (7), e0181167.

Korpilo, S., Virtanen, T., and Lehvävirta, S. (2017) Smartphone GPS tracking – inexpensive and efficient data collection on recreational movement, *Landscape and Urban Planning*, **157**, 608–617.

Newsome, D., Moore, S. and Dowling, R. (2012) *Natural Area Tourism: Ecology, impacts and management*, Bristol: Chanel View Publications.

Norman, P. and Pickering, C.M. (2017) Using volunteered geographic information to assess park visitation: Comparing three on-line platforms, *Applied Geography*, **89**, 163-172

Norman, P. and Pickering, C.M. (2019) Factors influencing park popularity for mountain bikers, walkers and runners as indicated by social media route data, *Journal of Environmental Management*, **249**.

Norman, P., Pickering, C.M. and Castley, G. (2019) What can volunteered geographic information tell us about the different ways mountain bikers, runners and walkers use urban reserves?, *Landscape and Urban Planning*, **185**, 180-190.

Oksanen, J., Bergman, S., Sainio, J. and Westerholm, J. (2017) Methods for deriving and calibrating privacy-preserving heat maps from mobile sports tracking application data. *Journal of Transport Geography*, **48**, 135-144.

Pickering, C.M., Rossi, S. and Barros, A. (2011) Assessing the impacts of mountain biking and hiking on subalpine grassland in Australia using an experimental protocol, *Journal of Environmental Management*, **92**(12), 3049–3057.

Rice, W., Mueller, J.T., Graefe, A., Taff, B. D. (2019) Detailing an approach for cost-effective visitor-use monitoring using crowdsourced activity data, *Journal of Park and Recreation Administration; Urbana*, **37** (2).

Rossi, S., Pickering, C., and Byrne, J. (2013) *Attitudes of local park visitors: assessing the social impacts of the South East Queensland horse riding trail network.* Brisbane: Department of Science, Information Technology, Innovation and the Arts.

Salas-Olmedo, M.H., Moya-Gómez, B., García-Palomares, J.C. and Gutiérrez, J. (2018) Tourists' digital footprint in cities: Comparing Big Data sources, *Tourism Management*, **66**, 13-25.

Santos, T., Mendes, R. N., & Vasco, A. (2016) Recreational activities in urban parks: Spatial interactions among users, *Journal of Outdoor Recreation and Tourism*, **15**, 1–9.

Strava (2020) Strava Metro. Available from: https://metro.strava.com/ [Accessed 5th August 2020].

6

7 Mobile Phone Tower Tracking

What this chapter will cover:

- The process of collecting big data from mobile phone companies.

- Methods that have been developed to differentiate tourists from locals using mobile phone data.

- The contributions that mobile phone data has made to understanding crowding, visitor numbers, event goer behaviour and repeat visitation.

- The limitations with this form of big data.

- The ethical issues associated with this form or data.

Introduction

Tracking tourists using mobile phone data involves collating mobile phone call detail records (CDR), that can determine travel patterns of mobile phone users. The size of the data involved in this style of research is enormous; Xiao, Wang, and Fang (2019) received 600 – 800 million records per day when they used mobile phone data from Shanghai, resulting in over 10 billion mobile phone trajectories. However, mobile phone data does not provide precise travel itineraries. Rather, the data is a series of time-space points, showing where mobile phone users were when they made or received calls or text messages. Inferences are required to determine which mobile phone users are tourists, and when they entered countries or regions. However, the ubiquity of mobile phone use and the size of the data sets available to researchers means that this form of data can be used as a proxy for accommodation and visitation (Xiao, Wang, and Fang, 2019; Ahas et al., 2008; Ahas et al., 2007). Many significant findings regarding travel behaviour have emerged from this technique, including understandings of the impacts of seasonality, the impacts of nationality, and the impacts of events. This chapter will review these findings as well as the challenges that arise from the use of this data.

How data is collected from mobile phone towers

Mobile phones are designed to send text messages or phone calls as radio waves from their antenna to a phone mast/base station and finally, to a receiving phone. Signals from the phone's antenna generally go to base stations with the strongest coverage, or those which are closest (Ahas et al., 2008). Base stations cover 'cells', which are areas of land that have been divided up, and the stations provide coverage to phones within their particular land area. If there are excessive amounts of users, phones may switch to a farther base station that is not being heavily used. The coverage of cells form the network (Ahas et al., 2008). When mobile phones cannot connect to a base station, they are regarded as being out of range.

There are a vast array of technologies used by different mobile phone networks, and these impact upon the strength of signals that mobile phones send to base stations. Typically, mobile phones can reach base stations 60 km away (Ahas et al., 2008). When a mobile phone is used to make a call or send a text message, their location coordinates are stored automatically in the memory files of the phone's mobile phone company. Each mobile phone has a random ID number, that stays with the phone and this is logged when the phone is used (e.g. text message, phone calls or use of the internet).

Mobile phone companies can track the location of phones that are registered with the company, plus those that are registered outside the country – called 'roaming' phones (Ahas et al., 2007). When 'roaming' phones enter a country, the mobile phone company can access information such as the phone's country of registration, when the phone entered and left the country, and the phone's random ID.

There are two types of tracking data that mobile phones can produce (Ahas et al., 2008). The first, and most commonly used in research, is 'passive positioning' which occurs when a mobile phone connects via a signal to mobile phone towers.

Zhao et al. (2018) argue that four situations create passive positioning of a mobile phone:

1. When a call is made or received;

2. When a text message is sent or received;

3. When the mobile phone changes position and switches to a different cell tower;

4. Via periodic reporting to mobile phone towers, outside of the previous three behaviors.

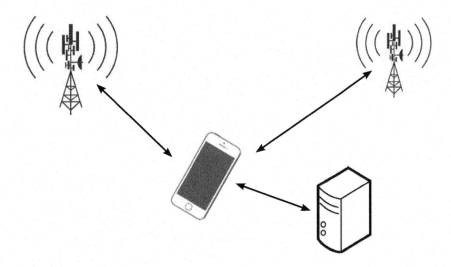

Figure 7.1: The process of collecting location-based mobile phone data.
When a mobile phone makes or receives a call or text message, the phone communicates with mobile phone towers. The mobile phone receives signals from towers that are within range. This information is then sent to a server which computes the position of the mobile phone, before sending this information back to the mobile phone.

The first two of these situations are referred to as CDR. The records contain information such as the identification number of the tower that the phone has connected to which can be used to determine the mobile phone's approximate location, the ID of the callers, the number of those that were called, the duration of the call and the type of activity e.g. making a call, sending and receiving an SMS, plus latitude and longitude coordinates of the signal (Ahas et al., 2008; Vanhoof et al., 2017; Toole et al., 2015; Xiao, Wang, and Fang, 2019).

The second type of positioning data that can be produced by mobile phones is called 'active positioning'. This form of data requires permission from the mobile phone owner and is not readily apparent in tourism research, thus will be given little attention in this chapter. Ahas et al. (2008, p. 470) defined it as:

> '...mobile tracing data in which the location of the mobile phone is determined (asked) with a special query using a radio wave... Active mobile positioning is used in emergency calls, "friend finder" and many other LBS applications.'

Methodological understandings that have emerged from this research

Because mobile phone data includes information only to do with the phone's registration origin and its location, researchers have had to design ways to determine which mobile phone users may be considered tourists. Home location during nighttime (that differs from the location where the phone was registered) is one method that has been used to determine locals from tourists. Xiao, Wang, and Fang (2019) defined home location being users' location between 12 midnight and 5 a.m., if it was the same for more than five days. They also defined workers in a park that they were studying as those whose locations were the same between 9 a.m. and 6 p.m. for more than five days.

Vanhoof et al. (2017) determined an algorithm to automatically define domestic tourists' destination. The algorithm assumed that the tourists' destination was close to the cell tower with the highest ratio of mobile phone activity and largest amount of days of usage during a domestic trip. The same research team also devised three options to filter out business trips from leisure travel. One option is to use mobile phone data from the summer months when business trips are less common. In their case, as the data was collected from France, they used data from July and August. A second option was to limit the window of acceptable trip durations by only using data of 8-15 days as this ensured a weekend was included, so it would be less likely that the trip was for business and more likely that the user was on a leisure trip. The authors noted an increasing trend for business and leisure trips to be combined (see Den Hoed and Russo, 2017), making it increasingly difficult to ensure that the data they were assessing was only made up on non-business travelers. Their final option was to assume domestic trips only included long distance trips beyond an 80 km radius from the home mobile phone tower.

Ahas et al. (2008) used a different methodology to try to filter out business trips from those of leisure travelers. They assumed that business people used their phones more frequently and pensioners less frequently. Those with higher usage were therefore assumed to be in a location for business, rather than leisure.

Methodological research has also been conducted to identify tourists who travel in a group. Zhao et al. (2018) developed an automated method called the Fine-Grained Travel Party Partition. Their data set included 12 million individuals in Xi'an, China and distinguished tourists as those who were in Xi'an during the study period but did not live in Xi'an and only spent a certain period of time there. They then assessed the behavioral sequences of tourists and extracted tourist with similar patterns to determine if they were travelling in groups.

A methodology for determining long distance trips has also been developed. Janzen et al. (2017) used the home-anchor model developed by Ahas et al. (2010) and identified a home cell tower for each user. Using a methodology similar to Vanhoof et al. (2017), they then defined the area within a radius of 80 km from the cell tower as their 'usual environment' and argued a long trip was when this radius was left and then returned to. They were able to develop a sequence of movement based on the first and last points that were located outside the 80 km radius. Following the application of this technique, the team argued that surveys underestimate the amount of people undertaking long distance trips, as well as the number of long-distance trips per person.

Conceptual understandings that have emerged from this research

A great variety of understanding pertaining to tourists' mobility has emerged from the use of this form of data. The first of these understandings relates to travel patterns. Raun et al. (2016) assessed two Estonian counties, and from the data could ascertain the number of counties visited by tourists, when the visits were made, the trip duration and the phone users' country of origin. This revealed connections and disconnections in space, between countries and also within local counties. They were able to determine how long visitors spent in locations and the impact of seasons on movement. They were also able to explore the relationship between home location and different travel patterns. However, they noted that research based on CDR is limited in its ability to asses geographical boundaries of a destination – while they were able to assess tourists' movement within government/municipal boundaries, they noted that these boundaries are not necessarily prominent in the mind of the tourist (Raun et al. 2016).

Seasonality has also been explored. During the high season, tourism spaces emerge, and this can be problematic in terms of overcrowding and the provision of infrastructure. The Estonian study of Ahas et al. (2007) had access to 9.2 million entries from 720,000 different roaming phones (classified as those registered in a country other than Estonia) over a one-year period. The study found that different nationalities of tourists used different spaces in Estonia across the seasons.

Event goers' behaviour has also been explored using this method. Nilbe, Ahas and Silm (2014) used this technology to track the travel distances of event goers in Estonia. They found that event tourists came from closer locations than regular tourists, thus the distance decay principle was found to be applicable for events. It also determined that events attract more visitors from more distant countries in the off-season (winter).

Data from this method has also been used in urban and transport studies (Ahas et al., 2008) to plan and manage traffic congestion. The correlation between this data and that collected through more traditional means has also been explored. Vanhoof et al. (2017) suggested that mobile phone data tends to correspond well with surveys and questionnaires. Similarly, while their study did not focus on tourists, Xiao, Wang, and Fang (2019) compared the spatial distribution of people's place of residence (this was based on where they slept) with the census of Shanghai and found it correlated well. Interestingly, some researchers argue that mobile phone tracking data often results in higher numbers of trips than official statistics (Ahas et al., 2008; Janzen et al., 2017).

Long distance trips have also been explored. Janzen et al. (2017) used mobile phone billing data from a period of 5 months to assess long distance travel journeys by tourists in France, from the mobile phone provider called Orange – this represented one-third of the French population. They attempted to identify five different reasons for travel – commuting, business, holidays, visiting friends/parents, and other reasons – using an algorithm. They looked at the data over a five-month period and identified home bases and the timing of when calls were made. The authors also developed and tested a predictive tool for behavioural trends in different types of travel.

One of the aspects that Vanhoof et al. (2017) explored was whether tourists called or sent more texts during domestic tourism trips. They found that calls and texts decreased. Moreover, their weekly usage patterns of usage changed when on holiday – they tended to use their phones less during the day and more on the weekend.

Zhao et al. (2018) undertook research in Xian in China. They examined the impact that party size has upon travel behaviours. They accessed mobile phone data from three phone companies in China. The use of three companies ensured they had a broad set of tourists. They collected the following data: the user encrypted ID; the position of the mobile phone tower that picked up the phone's signal; the time; and the SIM card origin. Zhao et al. (2018) used the data to identify five groupings:

1. Tourists travelling alone;

2. Travel parties with two in it (e.g. couples);

3. Travel parties with three to size in it (e.g. family travel);

4. Travel parties with 6-10 in it (e.g. small group travel)

5. Travel parties with more than 10 in it (large group travel).

They found that those in large groups do not travel as far and spend time at attractions that are closer to their accommodation than individuals and couples. They also found that those in small group sizes tend to demonstrate more diversified sequences and that family groups sought less novelty in the style of attractions they visited. For example, smaller groups made up of couples and individuals spent longer in Xi'an than tourists who travelled as family groups or tour groups.

Kuusik et al. (2011) developed a new approach of segmentation of repeat visitors. They looked at the call data from roaming mobile phone users in Estonia over a 4.5 year period to assess the movement patterns of international visitors to the country. They were able to assess the behaviour of repeat visitors (identified as mobile phone users who had large gaps between their call activities in Estonia), and categorised their travel into different levels of loyalty based on the length of time between revisits. They were also able to identify transit, long-term, one-day and other visitors within the repeat visitors that they studied, as well as event attendance activities. In doing so, the authors developed a new classification for segmenting repeat visitors.

Limitations

One of the most significant limitations of this method relates to the issue that whilst vast amounts of data can be accessed, very little is known about the users of the mobile phones. The data that is provided to researchers is series of time-space points that represent the location of the mobile phone when a call is made or received, or when a text is made or received. It also includes the mobile phone's identification number, country of origin, and its location. However this information does not provide any information to verify that those being tracked are indeed tourists (Vanhoof et al., 2017). Domestic tourists are especially hard to identify as they could be travelling away from their home location for leisure or business, or a combination of both.

This form of data collection is also limited as it is unable to answer research questions pertaining to tourists' previous travel history, motivation for travel, or their travel preferences. All of these factors have been identified as major influencers of travel behavior (Hardy, Biremboim and Wells, 2020). Raun et al. (2016) has noted that this form of research is unable to assess the social dimensions of destinations as the data does not allow researchers to understand how the destination is experienced over time.

Given that this method only locates phones when they are being used, behavior between usage is largely unknown. If someone does not use their phone, their presence is never recorded (Ahas et al., 2007). Many people who travel internationally limit their call usage in order to avoid international call charges. These travelers would be far harder to trace using this method – it is problematic to determine precisely when mobile phone users enter or leave a study area as they may have entered several days before making their first call and may have left several days after sending their last message.

Mobile phone tracking is also limited because the spatial accuracy of this method is limited by the density of cell towers over the study area (Versichele et al., 2014). Accuracy of tracking is dependent upon the location of towers – there are large numbers of towers in urban areas, but in many countries, they are far fewer in rural and remote areas (Vanhoof et al., 2017). In Estonia, research determined that around 50% of measurements were correct to within only 400 m in urban areas and only 2600 m in rural areas (Ahas et al., 2007).

The data is also limited to users of the mobile phone company that has provided the data and to the jurisdictions in which the company works (Nilbe, Ahas and Sil, 2014). For example, Axhausen, Schmid and Weis (2015) obtained data from Orange in France, but it was limited only to travel within France. This can, however, be overcome; Zhao et al. (2018) used data from three companies in China to circumvent this issue. It is also worth noting that while many antenna are visible to people, some mobile phone companies may choose to keep the location of their antenna secret from their competitors (Ahas et al., 2008), thus potentially compromising researchers' ability to access location-based data.

Mobile phone data is useful for large-scale studies, in terms of time and space. It is however limited in its capability to assess small-scale spatiotemporal behaviour, unless active tracking is utilised and the individual consent to be tracked (Versichele et al., 2014). Testing is also needed to ensure that assumptions regarding the types of tourist that mobile phones users appear to be. Studies have assumed that business travelers may be separated from normal travelers, because they use their phones more frequently when away from home, during business hours – e.g. Ahas et al. (2017). However, the same authors suggested that different nationalities use their phones more frequently regardless of whether they are traveling for leisure or business – for example, they assumed Scandinavians used their phones more frequently than central Europeans.

Finally, this form of mobility tracking is subject to the issue of 'spatial noise', as data from mobile phones can be problematic when tourist movement occurs in areas that are close to a country border. While a mobile phone user may not leave the country, their mobile phone may switch to a neighboring countries' network, thus inaccurately suggesting that that have crossed the border. A similar situation can occur in coastal areas – mobile phones that are used on board ships can be detected by mobile phone towers on land, so would be logged as tourists, when in fact they never set foot on land (Ahas et al., 2008).

Advantages

Mobile phone tracking data has many significant advantages. The first is that it provides vast amounts of data on movement through time and space, which may be accessed relatively cheaply (Ahas et al., 2008; Vanhoof et al., 2017; Raun et al., 2016). Mobile phone usage is now ubiquitous (often referred to as having high penetration rates) and the data that this research method produces has relatively good spatial resolution (Vanhoof et al., 2017). The data is often regarded as reliable in terms of understanding usage of infrastructure such as accommo-dation; Ahas et al. (2017) compared their mobile phone data set with accommodation statistics and found a good correlation.

Moreover, Janzen et al. (2017) found that this type of research is useful for studying long distance travel over a long period of time because there is no requirements for tourists to recall where they have travelled – this is a significant issue for surveys where recall has been documented as poor (Axhausen et al., 2015; Hardy et al., 2020; Shoval and Isaacson, 2010). Moreover, this form of data collection can be used to track the mobility of people who may be left out of traditional surveys, such as those who may not be literate or considered tradi-tional tourists. For example, Ahas et al. (2007) tracked fisherman who were not counted as tourists in traditional tourism databases. Further, Vanhoof et al. (2017) argues that while national tourism surveys can use arrivals data to estimate numbers, once in regional/rural areas it is harder to decipher tourists and understand how many people are visiting. Surveys that explore their behaviour once in these areas are also limited to tourists' recollection and are subject to responder bias. Silm and Ahas (2010) demonstrated that traditional data sources are not able measure short term and seasonal mobility patterns accurately. Therefore, it could be argued that the passive tracking approach means that there is no burden on users and no bias for involvement in the research (Vanhoof et al., 2017), apart from that which may be caused by the selection of the mobile phone provider.

Finally, this research offers the potential to understand how groups of tourists travel, and the social interactions of tourists and mobile phone users. Vanhoof et al. (2017) noted this research opportunity and suggested that it has rarely been conducted, but offers potential for future research.

Ethical issues

Ahas et al. (2007) wrote that the use of mobile phone data is a very 'sensitive issue' (p. 899). They argue that if the data is anonymized it is arguably no more intrusive than a census undertaken to determine occupancy in a hotel. However, the mobility aspect that emerges from mobile phone data usage is what adds an extra element of concern. The European Union's General Data Protection Regulation (GDPR) that came into full effect on the 25th of May, 2018 states that mobile phone companies may only use people's data if they have consented to it. They must opt in, not out.

Researchers must carefully abide by the ethical and privacy laws of their countries when undertaking this research. Moreover, the perception of the research should also be considered. While mobile phone data may be sourced legally and according to jurisdictional regulations, the tracking of people is not always seen to be morally justified. Ahas et al. (2008) use the case of China, where the tracking of movement of people has detracted from the country's reputation in the eyes of many potential travelers.

Summary

Mobile phone tracking allows researchers to access vast amounts of big data and assess the mobility of phone users. The ubiquitous use of mobile phones means this data may be considered to be very reliable, but the dearth of information connected to mobile phone data means that inferences must be made as to whether mobile phone users are tourists, precisely where they went (only calls and texts trigger locations to be revealed), and their travel motivations, such as business, leisure etc. There are also new ethical and privacy laws that must be taken into consideration when using this data, such as the GDPR regulations in the European Union that stipulate that mobile phone users must opt in before their data is shared.

Despite these limitations, this data offers many opportunities for researchers and significant conceptual understandings pertaining to tourist mobility have emerged from this form of data. Tourists' seasonal travel patterns, their behaviour as repeat visitors, and predictive tools that identify behavioural trends have emerged from the use of mobile phone tracking data. Provided the data is collected with individuals' informed consent and respects their privacy, this form of data offers may opportunities for research that focuses on tourists' mobility.

Key learnings from this chapter:

- Mobile phone tracking data can provide researchers with vast amounts of reliable data.

- This form of data has resulted in significant insights into flows of visitor numbers, crowding, and popularity of attractions.

- Researchers who use this form of data must often create algorithms to differentiate locals from non-local domestic visitors.

- There are difficulties in obtaining this form of data in many countries.

- Data that is sourced via mobile phone usage is non-continuous and so is unable to provide complete tracks of tourists' behaviour.

- This form of data provides only very limited socio-demographic data and no data that definitively determines tourists from non-tourists, nor data on tourists' preferences.

- Date should only be used from individuals who opt-in to have their mobile data used for research.

7

References

Ahas, R., Aasa, A., Mark, Ü., Pae, T. and Kull, A. (2007) Seasonal tourism spaces in Estonia: Case study with mobile positioning data, *Tourism Management*, **28**(3), 898-901.

Ahas, R., Aasa, A., Roose, A., Mark, U. and Silm, S. (2008) Evaluating passive mobile positioning data for tourism surveys: An Estonian case study data, *Tourism Management*, **29**(3), 469-486.

Ahas, R., Silm, S., Järv, O. Saluveer, E. and Tiru, M. (2010) Using mobile positioning data to model locations meaningful to users of mobile phones, *Journal of Urban Technology*, **17**(1), 3-27.

Axhausen, K. W., Schmid, B., and Weis C. (2015) Predicting response rates updated, *Arbeitsberichte Verkehrs-und Raumplanung*, 1063, IVT, ETH Zurich, Zurich.

Den Hoed, W. and Russo, A. (2017) Professional travellers and tourist practices, *Annals of Tourism Research*, **63**, 60–72.

Hardy, A. and Birenboim, A. and Wells, M. (2020) Using geoinformatics to assess tourist dispersal at the state level, *Annals of Tourism Research*, **82** .

Janzen, M., Vanhoof, M., Axhausen, K., Zbigniew, S. (2017) Estimating long-distance travel demand with mobile phone billing data, Conference Paper published in Proceedings of the 16th Swiss Transport Research Conference, Monte Verità/Ascona, May 18 – 20, 2016.

Kuusik, A., Tiru, M., and Varblane, U. (2011) Innovation in destination marketing: The use of passive mobile positioning for the segmentation of repeat visitors in Estonia, *Baltic Journal of Management*, **6**(3), 378-399.

Nilbe, K., Ahas, R., & Silm, S. (2014) Evaluating the travel distances of events visitors and regular visitors using mobile positioning data: the case of Estonia, *Journal of Urban Technology*, **21**(2), 91-107.

Raun, J. Ahas, R. and Tiru, M. (2016) Measuring tourism destinations using mobile tracking data, *Tourism Management*, **57**, 202-212.

Shoval, N. and Isaacson, M. (2010) *Tourist Mobility and Advanced Tracking Technologies*, New York: Routledge.

Silm, S., and Ahas, R. (2010) The seasonal variability of population in Estonian municipalities, *Environment and Planning A*, **42**(10), 2527–2546.

Toole, J.L., Herrera-Yaque, C., Schneider, C.M. and Gonzalez, M.C. (2015), Coupling human mobility and social ties, *Journal of the Royal Society Interface*, **12**(105), 1–14.

Vanhoof, M., Hendrickx, L., Puussaar, A., Verstraeten, G., Ploetz, T. and Smoreda, Z. (2017) Exploring the use of mobile phones during domestic tourism trips, *Netcom*, **31**, 335–372.

Versichele, M., De Groote, L., Bouuaert, M. C., Neutens, T., Moerman, I., and Van de Weghe, N. (2014) Pattern mining in tourist attraction visits through association rule learning on Bluetooth tracking data: A case study of Ghent, Belgium, *Tourism Management*, **44**, 67-81.

Xiao, Y., Wang, D., and Fang, J. (2019) Exploring the disparities in park access through mobile phone data: Evidence from Shanghai, China, *Landscape and Urban Planning*, **181**, 80-91.

Zhao, X., Lu, X., Liu, Y. Lin, J. and An, J. (2018) Tourist movement patterns understanding from the perspective of travel party size using mobile tracking data: A case study of Xi'an, China, *Tourism Management*, **69**, 368-383.

8 Tracking via Bluetooth and Wi-Fi

What this chapter will cover:

- The process of collecting big data via WiFi and Bluetooth.

- Methodological limitations on both methods in terms of capturing media access control (MAC) addresses.

- The contributions that these forms of data have made in understanding sequential visitor movement, crowding and its applicability both indoors and outdoors.

- The limitations with these forms of big data.

- The ethical issues associated with tracking via Bluetooth and WiFi.

Introduction

The technique of tracking tourists' mobility using Bluetooth and Wi-Fi technology has emerged as a reliable and viable option for tourism planners and researchers (Shoval and Ahas, 2016; Musa and Eriksson, 2012). Recent studies have employed Bluetooth to measure the time it takes for people to pass through security (Bullock et al., 2010); assess movement flows at festivals (Versichele et al., 2012); and explore movement through cities (Verischele, 2014). Bluetooth has also been used to track high speed movement, such as car and cyclists, whereas

Wi-Fi scanning, which takes a longer time to capture a signal, has been used to assess the flows of slower moving objects, such as tourists on foot, or other pedestrians (Abedi et al., 2013).

Tracking using Wi-Fi or Bluetooth offers researchers the ability to track vast amounts of data on movement in a relatively short period of time. Verischele et al., (2012) describes the scanning of Wi-Fi and Bluetooth signals as 'non-participatory' research because individuals are not required to sign up and participate to studies of this nature, nor are they aware they are being tracked. The advantage of this approach is that tourists do not change their behaviour because of the knowledge that they are being tracked.

This chapter will now review these forms of tracking technology, along with their advantages, limitations and ethical implications.

How tracking using Wi-Fi and Bluetooth works

All devices with Bluetooth and Wi-Fi functionality have a unique media access control (MAC) address (Kurkcu and Ozbay, 2017). These MAC addresses can be picked up by a Wi-Fi/Bluetooth scanners that are equipped with an SD memory card to store the data. Each form of tracking will now be addressed.

Bluetooth is known as a technology that uses low power, is robust and low cost (Song et al., 2008). It is estimated that between around 8-12% of mobile phone users can be detected using Bluetooth technology (Brennan et al., 2010). Interestingly, this form of data collection relies heavily on devices such as car-kits with Bluetooth capability that are in discovery mode – when they are trying to pair with a phone or another device (Kurkcu and Ozbay, 2017; Addinsight, 2017). Once a smart phone has paired with a car stereo, for example, it is no longer in discovery mode – this is the reason why Bluetooth scanning only picks up about 8-12% of total traffic. The device only has to be near the scanner for a few seconds to be discovered (Addinsight, 2017).

Wi-Fi scanning is similar in that it uses passive scanners that detect phones when they are looking for an access point. This happens about once every 60 seconds when Wi-Fi is enabled. Therefore in order to detect a Wi-Fi signal, phones need to be in the range of the scanner for around a minute – this requirement means that Wi-Fi tracking is most suited to pedestrians (Addinsight, 2017). For this reason, the technique of tracking via free Wi-Fi is very common these days – it is provided as a free service, but many providers use the service to collect data on movement through free Wi-Fi zones, provided users give consent when they sign on (see Figure 8.1).

Figure 8.1: A portable Bluetooth and WiFi scanner unit secured to a roadside pole. The battery operated sensors can collect data for several days at a time. This is TrafficBox from Smatstraffic, www.smatstraffic.com.

While it has been argued that Wi-Fi can capture data from phones from about 400m in optimal conditions (Fukuda et al., 2017), but most commonly both forms are cited as being able to reliably connect to phones or other devices from around 10-20 metres away (see Kurkcu and Ozbay, 2017; Oosterlincka et al., 2017). If scanners are carefully deployed to ensure good coverage, then the data can be much more granular than mobile phone tracking, thus facilitating detailed explorations of spatiotemporal behaviors (Versichele et al., 2014). Once scanners connect with Bluetooth or Wi-Fi, they collect data, including the MAC addresses of the phone, the date, time, and the location of the scanner (Arreeras et al., 2019). This data is then stored, or sent from the scanners onto servers in real time or in intervals.

8

Methodological insights from this method

Researchers using this method to track tourists have assessed the accuracy of this data. Oosterlincka et al. (2017) suggest that researchers should pre-test the method before commencing research. They determined the detection ratio by installing a video camera and manually counting people, then determining the percentage captured by a Bluetooth scanner – they calculated it was 9.46%. They also tested whether the location of scanners accurately represented individual's locations and found that phones could sometimes be detected 30 metres from the scanner, which means that actual locations may be hard to determine when using this method.

Researchers have also explored what may interfere with signals. Oosterlincka et al. (2017) found that while some scanners could penetrate through some walls, other load-bearing walls stopped signals from getting through. Oosterlincka et al. 2017 also found that metal shelving interfered with the scanners. They defined Type I errors as when the scanner detected someone coming into a store when in fact they were just walking by; and Type II errors as when devices entered the store but were not detected at all. The researchers ended up creating their own solutions – they wrapped their scanners in aluminium foil to create a faster decay of the signal – thus enhancing the workability of proximity principle and reducing the chances of tracking devices outside of the room of interest.

Kurkcu and Ozbay (2017) created algorithms to remove devices that were far away from the sensors (low signals suggested they were more than 15m from the sensor) and to remove non-mobile devices (these could be printers, staff phones, etc). They also created algorithms to remove those who appeared to be moving in circles or around the sensor (doing this removed double counting) – this was done by designing an algorithm with a cycle block of first 5 minutes – if MAC addresses were found in the first 5 minute block and then again the second, they were removed. The researchers then created an algorithm to assess pedestrians' flows between sensors – when the same MAC addresses were found at different sensors, that meant someone was moving. The algorithm also assessed the time spent between the sensors. Kurkcu and Ozbay (2017) used a Raspberry Pi to undertake the scanning – this is a small low cost computer commonly used in smart city projects (e.g. Leccese, Cagnetti and Trinca, 2014). Kurkcu and Oxbay (2017) were able to test the accuracy of the algorithm by comparing their outputs with manual crowd counts (also known as ground truth data).

Oosterlincka et al. (2017) also explored methods to determine the location of individuals. One way is to use the base station as the approximate location of the users, called the proximity principle. The other way is more complicated and involves the use of a complex method of triangulation and multilateration, plus 'fingerprinting' (where locations are worked out based on signal strength) to calculate individuals' locations based on multiple base stations.

There has also been research into the utilisation of the very large data sets that this form of data collection produces. Arreeras et al. (2019) used a style of machine learning called association rule mining to determine relationships between variables in very large data sets. In the context of tourism and using Wi-Fi, it allows planners to identify relationships between locations. Early adopters of association rule learning were Versichele et al. (2014).

Given that Bluetooth scanners pick up a range of devices, including GPS units and printers, researchers have been required to develop techniques that remove these devices, while retaining data from mobile phones. Verischele et al. (2014) developed a technique to do this using MAC addresses. They also had to remove some data noise for their dataset – for example, when a sensor was placed in a hotel that was near a parking lot, they discovered it was picking up patrons' devices as well as devices in cars in the parking lots. To overcome this they had to apply a time rule and remove devices that logged continuously for more than one hour. In another location they had to remove pedestrians passing by another hotel by adding a minimum time of 1 minute.

8

Understandings that have emerged from this method

In addition to methodological understandings that have emerged from the use of this method, many conceptual understandings have emerged in relation to tourists' mobility. Verischele et al. (2014) conducted one of the first studies of this type in tourism. They installed Bluetooth sensors at 29 locations around Ghent, Belgium, and assessed tourism movement through 14 tourist attractions over a 14 day period. The scanners (which had a range of around 10 metres) collected the MAC addresses of each device, plus the 'class of device' (e.g. phone, mp3 player, etc), and a timestamp. The researchers were able to use the unique MAC addresses to track the same device as it passed by different sensors.

Yoshimura et al. (2014) used Bluetooth to track visitors in the Louvre. They used the proximity method to track visitors' sequential movement. They installed seven sensors through the museum and placed them at the busiest attractions: e.g. the entrance, the Mona Lisa, the Venus de Milo and then Michelangelo's Dying Slave. The detection area was 20m long and 7m wide. They called each detection area a 'node'. The research team was also able to determine length of stay in nodes because a sensor was placed at the entry/exit. They were also able to determine travel times between nodes. They collected data over 24 days in 2010 – around 24,000 devices – and found that about 8.2% of visitors were able to be tracked. Significantly, their research found that the path sequences of long and short stay visitors was surprisingly similar. They argued that even when more time was available, visitors' paths tended to be selective. Thus, regardless of time, visitors seemed to go to the same places.

Bluetooth has also resulted in understandings regarding sequences of visitation, including differences in length of stay in locations between weekdays and weekends. Yoshimura et al. (2017) used Bluetooth to track pedestrians in the historical centre of Barcelona and found that they spent shorter periods of time in the district on weekends (especially on Saturday), but would visit a larger number of nodes within their limited time, compared to weekday pedestrians. Yoshimura et al. (2017) collated their data by placing a sensor in a metro station as an entry/exit point, then four more sensors through the historical centre, resulting in the tracking of over 4 million individual phones in a four-week period.

Advantages

Bluetooth and Wi-Fi scanning gives researchers the opportunity to access vast amounts of data and can be used in both indoor and outdoor locations (Verischele et al., 2014). It is particularly useful for what Oosterlincka et al. (2017) describes as 'uncontrolled' settings where people can move freely through space, such as mass events, within cities, shopping centres, airports and museums. A further advantage is that this form of data does not contain personal information (Verischele et al., 2014). It can also be implemented at very low cost and collates vast amounts of data, thus it offers researchers a very efficient research option.

Bluetooth scanning has an advantage because it is relatively rapid – scanners can pick up phones in discovery mode in a few seconds. Moreover, detection is reliable – if a phone has Bluetooth enabled and is within the scanners range for just a few seconds, it is likely it will be detected (Addinsight, 2017). In order to supplement deficiencies in either Bluetooth or Wi-Fi scanning (such as the length of time a Wi-Fi scanner can take to connect with a phone, or low rates of usage of Bluetooth), it is possible to combine both forms of scanning. Kurkcu and Ozbay (2017) implemented a duel scanning approach. This approach has also been taken by Lesani and Miranda-Mireno (2016) who collated Wi-Fi as a supplement to Bluetooth because they found that, at times, the detection rate for Bluetooth has been found to be as low as 2%. Since this study, the rates of usage of Bluetooth have risen significantly (Oosterlincka et al., 2017).

Limitations

While Wi-Fi and Bluetooth scanning offer researchers the opportunity to collate vast amounts of data relatively quickly and cheaply, both have limitations that should be addressed.

Bluetooth scanning

While this method is good for higher speed traffic and road environments, it is not so good for cyclists and pedestrian-only areas. This is because phone users may not have turned on the Bluetooth function on their phones; it is more likely that Bluetooth is on when individuals are in cars (Addinsight, 2017). Furthermore, Bluetooth only tracks about 5-10% of the traffic because a signal is only picked up when the phone is in discovery mode and not actually connected to another Bluetooth device (Addinsight, 2017). Moreover, one signal does not necessarily mean that one individual's movement has been tracked – a Bluetooth signals from a car may be tracking the movement of five people who are in a car, thus caution must be exercised when using this data to estimate the amount of mobility.

A further limitation of Bluetooth is that this type of data needs significant processing before being able to be used as suitable data – lots of 'noise' needs to be removed. One reason for this is that Bluetooth is used on a lot of devices, not just GPS car devices and smartphones (Verischele et al., 2014). Bluetooth tracking can also suffer from interference (Oosterlincka et al., 2017). For example, metal constructions can have an impact on the signal (Agostaro et al., 2004). Related to this, Bluetooth can pick up people that are not intended to be included – e.g. those in a parking lot adjacent to a hotel, pedestrians walking past the hotel, etc. Consequently, caution is needed to deciding where scanners should be located.

Wi-Fi scanning

Like Bluetooth, there are also limitations with Wi-Fi that must be taken into account. Wi-Fi works because phones send out signals around every 60 seconds to look for Wi-Fi access. However, potential data can be lost if individual phones are detected at site A, but not at site

B because the phone was in a car and its signal was not detected as it passed the scanner – this is especially an issue for high speed cars. Consequently, Wi-Fi is best used for research into slower moving mobility, such as pedestrians (Addinsight 2017). Oosterlincka et al. (2017) also noted that compared to Bluetooth, Wi-Fi has lower accuracy as Bluetooth is designed for short range wireless connections.

A further issue with Wi-Fi is that some phones generate random MAC address when they are in sleep mode, so their MAC addresses can change between scanners if the phone is in sleep mode. This means that individual phones cannot always be reliably traced for their movement (Addinsight 2017). This issue has been exacerbated by Apple whose introduction of iOS 8 brought in a new feature that uses a random MAC address for Wi-Fi connections, thus not allowing phones to be tracked via multiple scanners, unless the phone user has registered for the phone to be connected in order to access Wi-Fi from Wi-Fi providers.

When analysing data, Verischele et al. (2014) wrote that one of the limitations with both Bluetooth and Wi-Fi is the inability to distinguish between different types of tourists: domestic or international; business or pleasure, etc. However, this can be overcome by situating sensors in strategic places such as hotels, so that researchers can infer tourist type from where people are staying. A further limitation of both approaches is that scanners only have a small radius of 400m at most, thus many scanners are needed if accurate itinerary mapping is to be undertaken (Fukuda et al., 2017). Moreover, researchers are limited as they only know the scanner locations, not the locations of the phones. Thus, this method is problematic for those who wish to explore fine grained movement of tourists.

Ethical considerations of these approaches

The use of Wi-Fi and Bluetooth scanning, is, like all other methods, not without its issues in relation to privacy, ethics and consent. These have been noted by Yoshimura et al. (2017) and Oosterlincka et al. (2017) who warned that privacy concerns mean that non-participatory methods such as Wi-Fi and Bluetooth scanning should be viewed with great caution.

As with many other methods outlined in this book, the ethics of using these methods need to be considered in light of the researcher's institution and country of origin. For example, in Australia, the *National Statement on Ethical Conduct in Human Research 2007* (updated 2018) (National Health and Medical Research Council et al. 2018, p. 7) states that:

> *'Human research is conducted with or about people, or their data or tissue. Human participation in research is therefore to be understood broadly, to include the involvement of human beings through...access to their information (in individually identifiable, re-identifiable or nonidentifiable form) as part of an existing published or unpublished source or database.'*

Consequently, in Australia, according to this statement, consent would be required even though the data collected may be nonidentifiable. This is problematic when we consider that Bluetooth and Wi-Fi based data collection is being conducted on a large scale in order to monitor traffic, customer flows through shopping centres, and crowding at events. And despite this strict interpretation, in Tasmania, Bluetooth tracking is done on a regular basis in order to monitor traffic and adjust the traffic lights in the Central Business district during peak hour. Thus, it appears that, provided individuals' identity is not revealed, this method of research may be seen as acceptable under strict conditions.

In Europe, prior to the introduction of the General Data Protection Regulation (GDPR), there were already cases where companies were being monitored and, in some cases, prevented from collating data of this form. In France, the advertising company JCDecaux was prevented from tracking customers' smartphones as it was found to be collating the data via Wi-Fi but not taking measures to gain consent or anonymise the data (International Association of Privacy Professionals, 2020).

Again, despite instances of this method being banned in some locations, under the GDPR, there is a clause called 'Legitimate Interest' that allows data to be collated – it states that if the lead researcher has a legitimate reason for collating the data, then this method may be

deemed acceptable. In Article 6(1), the GDPR lists six possible principles for the processing of personal data. One of these, 6(1) f, states that
processing of data consent is gained, or if:

> '(d) processing is necessary in order to protect the vital interests of
> the data subject or of another natural person;

> (e) processing is necessary for the performance of a task carried out
> in the public interest or in the exercise of official authority vested in the
> controller.' (GDPR 2018; Article 6 (1)

In theory, it would be very hard to get consent from shoppers or
pedestrians before they activated their Wi-Fi. But according to the
above, administrative bodies could use Wi-Fi tracking when it is
really necessary to carry out a public task (point d and e) although
they would have to prove it is a necessity. For example, a commercial
business may be able to argue that they have a 'legitimate' business in
collecting tracking data on visitors to their store, but they would have
to prove it was also in the interests of its customers (Privacy Company,
2019). Furthermore, Recital 57 of the GDPR states that: '*The processing of
personal data for direct marketing purposes may be regarded as carried out for
a legitimate interest.*' (GDPR 2018; recital 47). Recital 50 also states that:
'*Further processing for archiving purposes in the public interest, scientific or
historical research purposes or statistical purposes should be considered to be
compatible lawful processing operations.*' (GDPR 2018; recital 50).

Some countries within the European Union have interpreted the
GDPR in a cautionary manner; in the Netherlands many municipalities
have suspended Wi-Fi tracking because of the GDPR and associated
difficulties involved in gaining consent from pedestrians. Given that
Wi-F scanning uses MAC addresses, which are linked to devices, there
is a chance individuals could be identified. However it should be noted
that this can be overcome – Kurkcu and Ozbay (2017) created a system
where only the last six digits of the MAC addresses were read and
stored. This ensured that the identity of those tracked could never be
traced.

At the time of writing, the European Union was developing ePrivacy
Regulations. These will be designed to provide more detail and to be
binding across all member states. The proposal is likely to have significant effects upon companies who use Wi-Fi and Bluetooth data.

Conclusion

Bluetooth and Wi-Fi tracking offers researchers the ability to collate vast amounts of data of pedestrians or those on bicycles or in cars, at a very low cost. The vast amounts of data can, in some instances, be viewed as a reliable proxy for movement. It has resulted in valuable insights in relation to traffic flow and congestion. However, it is a form of data collection that relies on passive tracking, therefore scanning of mobile phones can take place without having to involve research participants. New privacy legislation is increasingly becoming uncomfortable about the ethics of methods such as this. Therefore, researchers must be very cautious to ensure that if they do use this method, efforts have been taken to comply with their relevant jurisdictional and institutional requirements, as well as gain consent from participants, if possible.

Key learnings from this chapter:

- Data from Bluetooth and WiFi can provide researchers with vast amounts of data on visitor movement.

- This form of data has resulted in significant insights into flows of visitor numbers, traffic and crowding, plus sequential movement.

- This form of data is limited as it provides no socio-demographic data or data on tourists' preferences, therefore tourists cannot easily be differentiated from locals.

- Tracking can only be undertaken where sensors are located therefore this form of data is limited in its ability to continually track tourists.

- The lack of socio-demographic data obtained from this form of data collection means that it could be regarded as potentially less invasive.

- The use of this data has been treated with caution in many countries.

References

Abedi, N., Bhaskar, A., and Chung, E. (2013) Bluetooth and Wi-Fi MAC address based crowd data collection and monitoring: benefits, challenges and enhancement, In Proceedings of 36th Australasian Transport Research Forum, Brisbane, Queensland, Australia.

Addinsight (2017) Addinsight: Travel intelligence system. Available from: https://addinsight.com.au/ [Accessed 11th August, 2020]

Agostaro, F., Collura, F., Genco, F. and Sorce, S. (2004) Problems and solutions in setting up a low cost Bluetooth positioning system, *WSEAS Transactions on Computers*, **3**(4), 1102-1106.

Arreeras, T., Arimura, M., Asada, T. and Arreeras, S. (2019) Association rule mining tourist-attractive destinations for the sustainable development of a large tourism area in Hokkaido using Wi-Fi tracking data, *Sustainability*, **11**(14), 3967.

Brennan Jr, T. M., Ernst, J. M., Day, C. M., Bullock, D. M., Krogmeier, J. V. and Martchouk, M. (2010) Influence of vertical sensor placement on data collection efficiency from Bluetooth MAC address collection devices, *Journal of Transportation Engineering*, **136**(12), 1104–1109.

Bullock, D.M., Haseman, R., Wasson, J.S. and Spitler, R. (2010) Automated measurement of wait times at airport security: deployment at Indianapolis International Airport, Indiana, *Transportation Research Record*, **2177**(1), 60–68.

Fukuda, D., Kobayashi, H., Nakanishi, W., Suga, Y., Sriroongvikrai, K. and Choocharukul, K. (2017) Estimation of paratransit passenger boarding/alighting locations using Wi-Fi based monitoring: Results of field testing in Krabi City, Thailand, *Journal of the Eastern Asia Society for Transportation Studies*, **12**, 2151–2169.

General Data Protection Regulation (GDPR) (2018) General Data Protection Regulation Available at: https://gdpr-info.eu/ [Accessed 9 May 2018]

International Association of Privacy Professionals (2020) What the GDPR will mean for companies tracking location. Available from: https://iapp.org/news/a/what-the-gdpr-will-mean-for-companies-tracking-location/, [Accessed 4th April, 2020]

8

Kurkcu, A. and Ozbay, K. (2017) Estimating pedestrian densities, wait times, and flows with Wi-Fi and Bluetooth sensors, *Journal of the Transportation Research Board*, **2644**(1), 72-82.

Leccese, F., Cagnetti, M. and Trinca, D. (2014) A smart city application: a fully controlled street lighting isle based on Raspberry-Pi Card, a ZigBee sensor network and WiMAX, *Sensors*, **14**(12), 24408–24424.

Lesani, A. and Miranda-Moreno, L.F. (2016) Development and Testing of a real-time Wi-Fi–Bluetooth system for pedestrian network monitoring and data extrapolation, Presented at 95th Annual Meeting of the Transportation Research Board, Washington, D.C.

Musa, A.B.M. and Eriksson, J. (2012) Tracking unmodified smartphones using Wi-Fi monitors, In Proceedings of the 10th ACM Conference on Embedded Network Sensor Systems-SenSys, 12, Toronto, ON, Canada, 281–294

National Health and Medical Research Council, the Australian Research Council and Universities Australia (2018). *National Statement on Ethical Conduct in Human Research 2007 (Updated 2018).* Commonwealth of Australia, Canberra

Oosterlincka, D., Benoita , D.F., Baeckeb , P. and Van de Weghec, N. (2017) Bluetooth tracking of humans in an indoor environment: an application to shopping mall visits, *Applied Geography*, **78**, 55-65.

Privacy Company (2019) What does the GDPR say about WiFi Tracking?, Available from: https://www.privacycompany.eu/en/what-does-the-gdpr-say-about-wifi-tracking/ [Accessed 6 April, 2020].

Shoval, N. and Ahas, R. (2016) The use of tracking technologies in tourism research: the first decade, *Tourism Geographies*, **18**(5), 587-606.

Song, J., Lee, N.N., Chen, J.L., Dong, Y.F. and Zhao, Z. (2008) Design and implementation of intelligent transportation system based on GPRS and Bluetooth hybrid model, In Proceedings of International Conference on Automation and Logistics, 1381-1385.

Versichele, M., Neutens, T., Delafontaine, M. and Van de Weghe, N. (2012) The use of Bluetooth for analysing spatiotemporal dynamics of human movement at mass events: A case study of the Ghent festivities, *Applied Geography*, **32**(2), 208–220.

Versichele, M., De Groote, L., Bouuaert, M. C., Neutens, T., Moerman, I. and van de Weghe, N. (2014) Pattern mining in tourist attraction visits through association rule learning on Bluetooth tracking data: A case study of Ghent, Belgium, *Tourism Management*, **44**, 67-81.

Yoshimura, Y., Sobolevsky, S., Ratti, C., Giradin, F., Carrascal, J., Blat, J. and Sinatra, R. (2014) An analysis of visitors' behavior in The Louvre Museum: a study using Bluetooth data, *Environment and Planning B: Planning and Design*, **41**(6), 1113-1131.

Yoshimura, Y. Amini, A., Sobolevsky, S., Blat, J. and Ratti, C. (2017) Analysis of pedestrian behaviors through non-invasive Bluetooth monitoring, *Applied Geography*, **81**, 43-51.

8

9 Tracking via Bespoke Research Apps

What this chapter will cover:

- The technique of collecting data from bespoke apps that have been designed to track tourists and collect their socio-demographic data.

- The contributions that this form of data have made to understanding dispersal, how different segments of tourists travel and the factors that influence tourists' movement through time and space.

- The methodological advantages and limitations of this expensive yet highly detailed spatio-temporal method.

- The ethical advantages of this form of data which requires informed consent.

Introduction

In the past ten years, several apps have been developed by research teams with the specific intention of tracking tourists. These apps contain user interfaces that explicitly communicate the function of these apps. They differ to apps, websites and social media sites described in the previous chapters, because the primary function of their user interface is to track and understand the characteristics of tourists. This form of tracking produces highly detailed, tourism-specific data which can be of great value to tourism researchers. But it is not without its challenges. These will be explored in this chapter.

How bespoke apps work

Apps that have been designed to track tourists' movement generally contain three elements. They contain:

1. A user interface that may or may not have value-adds such as maps and destination information;

2. A survey function that collects socio-demographic and behavioural data from app users – multiple surveys may be used, such as entry and exist surveys, or location based surveys that 'pop-up' at pre-determined locations;

3. A tracking function, whereby location-based data is stored by the app and then sent to a server or dashboard for cleaning and visualisation.

Bespoke tracking apps have to take a variety of factors into consideration during their design. The first is that the app needs to be able to maximise tracking, therefore it is important that users are guided through the process of enabling location-based tracking and encouraged to select the option that allows ongoing tracking (Figure 9.1).

The next factor that bespoke apps must consider is that data needs to be collected at all times, on different brands of mobile phones. Apps of this nature use location-based data that is sourced from the mobile phone's communication with satellites. Commonly used satellite systems that phones communicate with include the US GPS, Russian GLONAS, and EU Galileo. Well-designed bespoke apps will collect the GPS coordinates, even when the mobile phone is out of cell tower range, and then once they detect the mobile phone has reception or is within Wi-Fi range, will send the data to a server for cleaning and analysis.

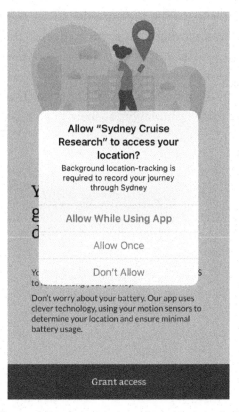

Figure 9.1: Instructions for enabling location-based tracking on the Tourism Tracker bespoke tracking app

Bespoke apps must also consider battery life, as the collection of location-based data can drain battery life very quickly. Researchers must balance data granularity with power saving. In the case of the bespoke app called Tourism Tracer, a decision was made to set the collection of data to ten metres every 2 seconds. This granularity allowed tourists' movement to be tracked with high detail, without impacting on the battery life of the host mobile phone (Hardy et al., 2017).

A further functionality that is required is usability. Bespoke apps rely on users providing personal and potentially sensitive information to the researcher. The app design must be user friendly and ensure that users are confident in its ability to store their data ethically and safely. Some apps provide incentives to users in return for them providing their data in the first instance (Hardy et al., 2017). Similarly, given that bespoke apps can track tourists' movement for multiple days and potentially very long periods of time, there is also a necessity for bespoke apps to maintain the participation of the tourists that they are tracking. It is important that participants feel that the app is worth their while to use, particularly when they are travelling (Anuar and Gretzel, 2011). In one incarnation of its application, Tourism Tracer provided an incentive, in the form of a map of their travels through the destination, to tourists upon completion of their final survey for this very reason (Figure 9.2).

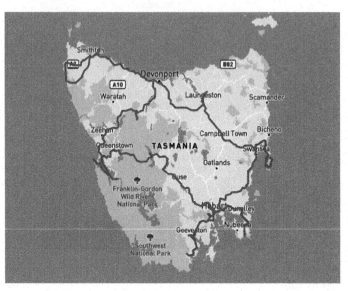

Figure 9.2: Incentive provided to participants, in the Tourism Tracker study – of a map of their travels through a destination.

In a further application of the technology, a free coffee voucher could be activated upon completion of the final survey.

An additional functionality of tracking apps is that, due to their bespoke nature, they may be designed to sync with other data sets. In the case of Tourism Tracer, some survey questions were designed in the same format as the Tasmanian Visitor Survey, so that the data could be synced and visualised on the data dashboard. The location-based data was also synced with the Australian Tourism Data Warehouse data, which contains the GPS coordinates of a large majority of tourism businesses in the country. This allowed for automated visualisations of the exact businesses that tourists went to, and the flow of movement between businesses (Figure 9.3).

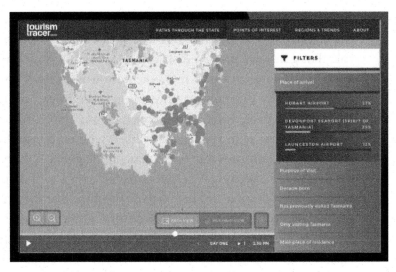

Figure 9.3: The Tourism Tracer dashboard, with questions that synced to existing data sets

Finally, a significant functionality of apps of this type is the ability to visualise this data in close to real time. Visualisation is possible when using other data sets such as surveys, but can often be hampered because they are being sourced from a second or third party provider where delays may occur. In the case of bespoke apps that are designed by research teams, there is the option for data dashboards to be built that visualise data in real time, or close to real time. In the case of Tourism Tracer, a polygon was created around the island state of Tasmania and as soon as tourists left the state, their data was added to the visualisation on the dashboard. This delay ensured a level of safety for tourists so that users of the dashboard could not locate them in real time.

9

Conceptual findings that have emerged from bespoke tourism tracking apps

The bespoke nature of this form of tracking has resulted in a variety of significant conceptual findings related to tourists' behaviour and the impact of tourism upon urban and regional economies. This is in part due to the ability of app technology to be able to track over multiple days and across entire destinations, thus eliciting detailed insights into spatial and temporal movement patterns.

Recent comparative work by Raun, Shoval and Tiru (2020), which tracked arrivals in Estonia and Israel, have demonstrated the major role that gateways play in distributing tourist flows within countries. Their research found that most of the tourist activity takes place in close proximity to gateways, thus, if pressure from a concentration of tourism is to be reduced, additional gateways must be added. These findings concur with Hardy et al. (2020) who demonstrated gateways play a very significant role in influencing dispersal and that if tourists enter and exit through different gateways, they will disperse farther in terms of both area and the farthest distance that they travel. Hardy et al. (2020: p. 12) also found that several other factors that *'influence dispersal on a small scale also influence dispersal on a state-wide scale. These include length of stay, familiarity of destination and transport.'*

In Korea, Yun and Park (2015) tracked tourists for five days while in the confined space of a festival. The festival-goers were asked to download a specialised GPS fitness and tracking app called Tranggle GPS. 95 people agreed to participate with 65 reporting back their data at the end of five days – they had to upload their tracking records to the researchers for analysis. No socio-demographic data was collected via the app, but rather via personally administered questionnaires. The research yielded fascinating insights – the temporal and spatial density analysis of festival visitors' behaviour revealed limited socio-economic benefits of this festival upon the local economy, plus very limited inter-action between tourists and local residents. Thus, the festival did not have the trickle-down effect on the local economy that was anticipated (Yun and Park, 2015).

In their study of small historic townships, McKercher, Hardy and Aryal (2019) challenged the preconceived notions of special interest tourists. The research team assessed a heritage town and found that each segment of tourist (defined by their stated trip purpose) behaved differently in the heritage township and their behaviour showed distinct preferences for differing bundles of attractions. But, contrary to expectations, the heritage-motivated and visiting-friends-and-relatives (VFR) segments of tourists did not have the strongest interaction with the historical township – in fact these groups stayed the least amount of time in the town while those whose stated preference was for experiencing wilderness and wildlife attractions stayed the longest in the town. The study also illustrated the significance of different types of space in small townships and the need for destination managers to consider them. These included geographic space which relates to the layout of the town (such as its linear nature and a node in the town centre); mental space, which is the locations that tourist found attractive and tended to visit; and social space, which is the route that tourists tend to take.

Research using bespoke apps has also resulted in an understanding of travel patterns. Building upon McKercher and Lau's (2008) early work that conceptualised travel patterns, the work of Hardy et al. (2020) showed that when tourists stay longer in destinations, their travel patterns change from one which may be regarded as a hub and spoke pattern to one which could be regarded as a circular or touring pattern.

Methodological findings from this approach

A variety of methodological findings have emerged from this technique. Most significantly is that this technique has demonstrated the ability for technology to track tourists for the entire duration of their stay in destinations. Unlike others that are constrained by limited sensor range or incomplete data, this method offers the opportunity to produce continuous tracking data for individuals, thus yielding highly detailed behaviour data.

However, there are also some challenges with this approach. One of these relates to the issue of recruitment. Resistance to being tracked has stalled a variety of studies that have attempted to use this technique (e.g. Thimm and Seepold, 2016), resulting in some researchers using incentives to encourage participation (e.g. Yun and Park, 2015). Incentives can be offered at different stages during the research process, such as: immediately after the app is downloaded; during participants' journeys; and following completion of their required app activities. For example in the case of the research of Hardy et al. (2017), participants were sent a map of their entire journey upon completion of an exit survey that was required to be completed before they left the island

9

state of Tasmania. In a study in Israel, tourists were approached at the Ben Gurion Airport and offered a free smartphone with free local use in exchange for their participation in a study (Raun, Shoval and Tiru, 2020). What has been found is that careful consideration of the possible points at which tourists can pull out of research that uses apps must be undertaken – it is likely that incentives that are strategically timed to be made available at these times will help participation.

Preliminary research by Hardy and Wells (2019) showed that different types of incentives of tourist tracking are likely to create different levels of buy-in. The researchers conducted their study in Skåne, Sweden over three phases of recruitment. During each phase, 100 people were approached randomly, and offered one particular incentive. The three incentives that were tested included:

1. A digitalised journey history of the tourists' travels in Southern Sweden, in the form of a map;

2. A digitalised journey history plus a powerbank that could be used to recharge electronics; and

3. A digitalised journey history plus a discount at a local store.

In the case of the first phase, where the journey history map alone was offered, the incentive was only available through the app after tourists had participated, as it contained a visualisation of the results of tracking their trip. In the case of the second and third phase, the incentive was given to the tourists after they had installed the tracking app.

The research assessed the reactions of tourists to the incentives, along with the propensity to stay in the study. Four stages, referred to as hurdles, were identified for the recruitment process:

1. Potential participants must be willing to be approached by recruiters;

2. Potential participants must agree to download an app onto their phone;

3. Potential participants must set up the app and enable tracking, plus complete a survey;

4. Potential participants must maintain location-based tracking for at least 12 hours.

The following results emerged:

- Those tourists who were offered the journey history plus the powerbank, and those who were offered the journey history plus a discount incentive, cleared the four aforementioned hurdles in similar rates.

- Tourists who were offered only their journey history were distinctly different; only 15% of those who agreed to participate went on to fill out a survey and start tracking.

- 80% of tourists who were offered the journey history map plus a powerbank, and agreed to participate, and 67% of tourists who were offered the journey history map plus a discount, and agreed to participate, successfully started tracking.

- Despite being offered very few incentives, tourists who were offered only a digitised journey history stayed in the study for the longest period of time if they cleared the previous three hurdles (Figure 9.4).

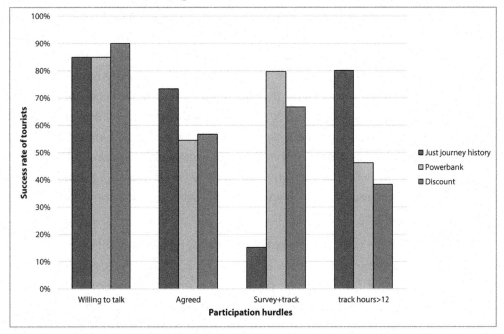

Figure 9.4: Incentives and hurdles to participation

This research also revealed that tourists in the 18-29 and 30-39 age groups consistently agreed to take part more than 50% of the times they were approached, while other age groups mostly declined. Beyond the initial consent, the research also revealed that while older tourists were more likely to say no initially, tourists aged 70 or older ended up with the highest percentage of long tracks.

Research has also explored the difference between two methods of app usage. Hardy, Aryal and Wells (2019) used two techniques. First they 'staged' a fleet of study phones that had a research app pre-loaded onto them. Following this they asked participants to download a standalone app onto their own mobile phone device. When comparing the techniques, they found that study phone users had greater engagement with the app in terms of survey completion. Moreover in the first year of the study that used staged mobile phones, the data had far superior traces of travel. A marked deterioration occurred in the second year, when the phones aged and their ability to gather location based data appeared to decline.

Following this, the second technique that Hardy, Aryal and Wells (2019) utilised involved a standalone app that required self-recruitment. This yielded a high number of participants, but many did not activate the app's tracking function or complete the survey. However, when they did activate the tracking, the standalone app produced consistently high-quality traces of tourists' travel. This was probably due to improvements in the tracking technology that occurred after the use of the staged phones. Significantly, this study also demonstrated that recruiters play an important role in assisting participants to set up standalone apps so that they can accurately track and collect demographic data. It also demonstrated the need for all equipment to be updated regularly to respond to changes in technology and tracking regulations.

Recent work has also explored the application of different dispersal measurement methods. Currently, the goal to disperse tourists beyond cities and into regional areas, to maximise the economic benefits to regions whilst minimising overcrowding, is very significant to many tourism organisations. Hardy, Birenboim and Wells (2020) compared four different dispersal measurement tools to determine the research questions and tracking methods that they were most suited to. Traditionally, tourism agencies have tended to use ratios, whereby a geographical line is created and tourists who venture beyond the line (e.g. a city boundary) are regarding as having dispersed (as an example, see Tourism Government and Tourism Industry Council of Tasmania, 2015). The authors determined that measures such as this, while coarse in detail, are appropriate for data sets that are produced from surveys, but are not suitably fine grained for studies that use bespoke tracking apps with locations based technology.

A second tool for measuring dispersal is the maximum linear distance measure, whereby the tourists dispersal is measured by the two most distant GPS points (also known as Euclidean distance) that a tourist has travelled. This method of measurement was determined as being useful for studies that utilise bespoke apps and location-based tracking and therefore appropriate when researchers wish to assess tourists' willingness to overcome space friction/distance decay. A third tool they assessed was the use of a standard deviation ellipse, also termed an 'activity space indicator'. This tool assesses the area covered by tourists, while also accounting for time and space measurement and was found to be extremely useful for data produced by bespoke tracking apps. A fourth and final tool that was used was a cumulative distance indicator which determines the total distance travelled by tourists while on their holiday. This tool was also found to be useful for data produced by tracking apps, given its requirements for both spatial and temporal data.

Finally, the involvement of stakeholders in the design of bespoke apps, in order to maximise knowledge transfer and impact, has been explored. The Tourism Tracer project utilised a staged approach to design and implement their app, which was informed by the elaboration likelihood approach. The first stage involved diagnosing the problem that required solving and possible forms of action to solve this problem, In their case it was the lack of location based data that determines tourists' exact behaviour, and a desire to overcome this. During this stage, stakeholder consultation was conducted, along with a series of seminars, to flesh out possible solutions. An advisory board was also convened, to ensure that the research team would create *"relevant, engaging and impactful research for the Tasmanian community"* (Hardy, Vorobjovas-Pinta and Eccleston, 2018). It also involved assembling a team of researchers with specialist research skills, including those who were deemed to be 'academically bilingual' – able to communicate highly technical research terms in an understandable manner to the broader tourism industry. The second stage, referred to as the 'action taking' stage involved branding the project (hence the name 'Tourism Tracer'), media to encourage implementation of the app, and blogs, media, and YouTube videos to report preliminary results. The third stage involved evaluation and sharing of the data. This stage resulted in an easy to use data dashboard that communicated the results, and synced the data with reputable sources, which encouraged both peripheral and central cues. Embedding an elaboration likelihood approach into all the stages of the project demonstrated the ability to enhance the process, uptake, and knowledge transfer of new technology (Hardy et al., 2017). The project demonstrated that co-created research design is well suited to disruptive technology that involves multiple stakeholders. Moreover, a co-creation approach can help to further innovative approaches and outcomes (Eccleston, Hardy and Hyslop, 2020).

Limitations

While the use of bespoke tourism tracking apps offers the opportunity to collect context specific and highly detailed datasets on tourists' movement, they are not without their limitations. Early work in this field encountered significant resistance to this technique from potential study participants. Thimm and Seepold (2016) developed an app to track tourists' movement around Lake Constance in Germany. Their app included an incentive that they felt would be attractive – a travel diary and a calorie burning function. However while they found that 65 tourists expressed interest in their study, only two tourists downloaded the app and one activated the tracking mode, only to deactivate it shortly afterwards.

The Tourism Tracer app appeared to overcome this resistance (discussed above in methodological advances), but encountered other forms of resistance to tracking. In a study conducted in Skåne, Sweden, Hardy and Wells (2019) encountered initial higher resistance to tracking amongst those from Germany, compared to those from Scandinavia. Interestingly, of those who did agree to participate, they found that those from Sweden and Germany were more likely to continue in the study for the duration, compared to those from Denmark who had a high drop-out rate, despite agreeing to participate. In a more recent study, Hardy and Wells (2020) found significant resistance from cruise ship passengers who were asked to track their movement through Sydney, Australia, at the end of their cruise. This resistance warrants further investigation but it appears that end of trip fatigue may play a significant role in rates of participation. Furthermore, Yun and Park (2015) raised the concern that getting people to download an app meant that only a limited demographic would be prepared to participate. Caution is needed to assess the sample of participants and ensure that responder bias does not negatively impact the data quality.

Related to this is the issue of consent. The decision to recruit participants presents researchers with the opportunity to be explicitly clear about the function of the app and avoid the potential for informed consent to be overlooked. The majority of studies that have used a bespoke app have utilised recruiters, therefore the potential for participants not being aware that they are being tracked is minimised. However, if recruiters are not being used, it is important that researchers and designers pay great attention to the design to ensure that participants understand that they are providing their location-based data for research purposes and that it will be protected and stored in accordance with the relevant ethical requirements.

A further limitation of this method is the cost required to develop a bespoke app. More significantly, this method may require recruitment of participants and this is where significant costs may be incurred. While there are cases, such as the latter part of the Tourism Tracer program (Hardy, Birenboim and Wells 2020) where physical recruiters are not required (signs sufficed to encourage tourists to download the app), the majority of studies using this technique have relied upon recruiters and therefore are relatively costly forms of data collection.

9

Battery life is also an issue that developers of bespoke tracking apps must consider. In their Korean study, Yun and Park (2015) noted concerns about the battery life of mobile phones; their recruiters were instructed to only select participants that had good battery life on their phones in order to ensure good quality data. In the case of Tourism Tracer, the battery life of participants' phones was not considered during recruitment because the study stretched over multiple days. Rather, battery life was considered during the design of the app and the tracking was 'slowed down' in terms of its time between point capture, to decrease the likelihood that the app would drain the mobile phone battery.

A further limitation of this method relates to what may be called 'points of departure'. Unlike other forms of tracking, such as that which is done via mobile phone towers, the collection of social media data, or via the internet, bespoke apps require participants to opt in and consequently there are multiple opportunities at different times for them to opt out. For example, participants can react positively to recruiters request to download an app and then not do it. Alternatively, they may download the app but not enable location based tracking. Or they may download the app, enable location tracking and then delate the app immediately afterwards. They may keep the app going for part – or all of their journey. Thus, there are multiple points of departure with this method – more so than for many other tracking methods. The challenge for researchers is to recognise these potential points of departure during the app design phase and, using a range of communication tools and non-coercive behavioural changing incentives, minimise the likelihood of points of departure by tourists.

Designers of bespoke apps must consider not only battery life, but must also consider memory. This form of data collection collates vast amounts of data and research has shown that many people's phones often have only limited memory left (Berkowski, 2014). The design of apps must take this into account and be able to deal with this. The Tourism Tracer app takes into account memory at two points – the app was designed to be as small as possible in terms of size (it has been applied to various destinations but generally it is around 29-35 megabytes), so that users are be able to install it on their own phones.

Second, the app is designed to send the location-based and survey data to servers as soon as the mobile phone is was within Wi-Fi range, or within range of a mobile phone tower. This significantly reduces memory storage.

Finally, bespoke apps that are designed to track must be designed so that they abide by the rules set by the iTunes and Google Play stores. Both stores require that app developers must justify why apps seek to undertake location-based tracking and also abide by regulations on when tracking can occur (e.g. 'only once', 'while use the app' or 'not at all'). These regulations change regularly so app developers must ensure they stay abreast of these shifts in policy.

Conclusion

The development of bespoke tourist tracking apps has created the opportunity to collect highly nuanced, detailed and context-relevant data for destinations. The bespoke nature of these apps means that data may be synced with existing data sources and that consent and ethical research practices can be easily dealt with. The development of apps such as these has led to unprecedented insight into how tourists use gateways, disperse, package their choices and in doing so, has both confirmed and challenged tourism behaviour theories.

Methodologically, apps such as these have demonstrated their ability to collect data efficiently, particularly since issues such as battery life and data storage have been overcome. Moving forward, one of the greatest challenges for bespoke apps is that their design is deemed acceptable by platforms such as iTunes and the Google Play store, who are increasingly placing regulations on tracking apps and their functionality. The frequency of changes to these regulations requires app developers to stay abreast of changes and to ensure regular app updates occur.

The highly ethical and upfront nature of the technique means that participants are made aware of the desire to track behaviour and this knowledge means that recruitment can be difficult. The Cambridge Analytica crisis heightened societies' awareness of tracking and

9

arguably created increased resistance to the phenomena. Conversely, the COVID-19 pandemic highlighted the role that tracking apps can play in assisting societies and tourism destinations in general. The challenge for researchers moving forward will be to assure potential participants that the use of bespoke apps may be relied upon as they provide a heightened level of reliability in terms of obtaining consent, and ethical data storage and management. This, along with their ability to collect bespoke data, remains their most significant advantage to researchers, as well as participants.

Key learnings from this chapter:

- Bespoke apps offer researchers the ability to tailor the collection of data to their research needs.

- This form of data collection allows for real time spatiotemporal and socio-demographic data that can be collected over a long period of time.

- Bespoke apps have resulted in significant insights into factors that influence dispersal, differences in travel between travel segments and the consumption of destinations by different segments of tourists.

- This form of data faces is not without challenges – tourists are required to download apps onto their personal devices and enable location-based tracking.

- Bespoke apps offer the ability for researchers to undertake research in an ethical manner, as consent must be gained from participants.

References

Anuar, F., and Gretzel, U. (2011) Privacy concerns in the context of location-based services for tourism, in ENTER 2011 Conference, Innsbruck, Austria.

Berkowski, G. (2014) Press release. Available from: http://www.prweb.com/releases/2014/12/prweb12395977.htm [Accessed 10th October, 2016]

Eccleston, R., Hardy, A. and Hyslop, S., (2020) Unlocking the potential of tracking technology for co-created tourism planning and development:

Insights from the Tourism Tracer Tasmania project, *Tourism Planning & Development*, **17**(1), 82-95.

Hardy, A., Aryal, J. and Wells, M. (2019) Comparing techniques for tracking: the case of Tourism Tracer in Tasmania, Australia, *E-review of Tourism Research*, **16**(2/3), 84-94.

Hardy, A. and Birenboim, A. and Wells, M. (2020) Using geoinformatics to assess tourist dispersal at the state level, *Annals of Tourism Research*, **82,** Article 102903.

Hardy, A., Hyslop, S., Booth, K., Robards, B., Aryal, J., Gretzel, U. and Eccleston, R. (2017) Tracking tourists' travel with smartphone-based GPS technology: a methodological discussion, *Information Technology & Tourism*, **17**(3), 255-274.

Hardy, A. and Wells, M. (2019) *Recruiting Tracking Participants in Skåne, Sweden.* Unpublished report for Tourism Skåne.

Hardy, A., Vorobjovas-Pinta, O. and Eccleston, R. (2017) Enhancing knowledge transfer in tourism: an Elaboration Likelihood Model approach, *Journal of Hospitality and Tourism Management*, **37,** 33-41

Hardy, A. and Wells, M. (2020) *Preliminary results of the pre-COVID travel movements of cruise ship tourists in Sydney, Australia.* Unpublished report for Ports Authority of New South Wales.

McKercher, B., Hardy, A. and Aryal, J. (2019) Using tracking technology to improve marketing: insights from a historic town in Tasmania, Australia, *Journal of Travel and Tourism Marketing*, **36** (7), 823-834.

McKercher, B. and Lau, G. (2008) Movement patterns of tourists within a destination, *Tourism Geographies*, **10**(3), 355-374.

Raun, J., Shoval, N. and Tiru, M. (2020). Gateways for intra-national tourism flows: measured using two types of tracking technologies. *International Journal of Tourism Cities*, **6**(2), 261-278.

Thimm, T. and Seepold, R. (2016) Past, present and future of tourist tracking, *Journal of Tourism Futures*, 2 (1), 43-55.

Yun, H., and Park, M. (2015) Time–space movement of festival visitors in rural areas using a smart phone application, *Asia Pacific Journal of Tourism Research*, **20**(11), 1246-1265.

9

10 Tracking Tourists' Mobility via the Internet

What this chapter will cover:

- The technique of collecting big data from the internet, where digital traces allow the approximate location of internet users to be tracked.

- The variety of means by which this form of data can be collected.

- The conceptual findings that this form of data has facilitated, including predictions of tourists' behaviour and insights into tourists' behaviour.

- The ethical issues that this form of big data can raise.

Introduction

Tracking tourists' mobility and migratory patterns may be conducted by collating their digital footprints via the web. Data of this sort may be sourced via apps such as Google Maps, or websites that collate IP numbers and their proximity to mobile phone towers. It may also be collected via big datasets such as ticketing websites, via mini programs such as those used by WeChat, and via non-big data sources such as blogs.

This form of location-based tracking is a highly efficient and cost-effective means of understanding where consumers are located. The devastating impacts of the COVID-19 pandemic upon the tourism industry have clearly indicated the potential for tracking via the internet to assist the tourism industry. Google's analytical data that was released publicly in March 2020 provided an excellent example of this – both in terms of the insights that can emerge from data of this type, and consumers' perceptions of the ethics of this form of data.

This chapter will explore the technique, including the types of location-based data that can emerge from websites, the conceptual learnings that have emerged from this technique, and, importantly, the ethical implications of this form of data.

How tracking via the Internet works

Tracking consumer behaviour on the internet has become big business. Research that tracks mobility via the web has largely been contained to the commercial sector, but examples do exist in academia. The use of internet data and big data requires highly technical economics and forecasting methodological skills. These will not be detailed here, rather the capability of the data in terms of its ability to determine tourism mobility and movement will be explored.

Tracking via the internet may be done in a number of different ways:

- **First-party data**: this form of data has been collated by a business and reveals specific information on the business's existing customers;

- **Second-party data**: is collected by one business and then shared with another – for example one business collects tracking data on its consumers and then shares it with another business;

- **Third-party data**: is collected by businesses – called data aggregators – who intend to sell the information. This data can be useful for identifying new customers as well as tracking current customers. Examples of data aggregator companies include Mobile Walla and peer39. It is important to note that the data that tourism organisations buy from data aggregators is not necessarily unique – the same data can be sold by the data aggregating company to multiple organisations (Mobilewalla, 2020).

Most commonly, research that is publicly available is sourced from first party data. Second and third party data tends to be kept as commercial assets, and only shared in confidence. An example of first party data is the use of cookies, that can be used to track and collate online behaviour. Cookies allow websites to recall individuals' behaviour on websites at the time of their visit – so consumers can add to their shopping cart purchases – (called 'session cookies'), and also long-term recollection of consumers' browsing histories (called 'tracking cookies'). Cookies may be used to collate purchasing data and make predictions on future purchase decisions, plus they can assess how consumers move through cyberspace, *but* they cannot assess how those who make purchases move through physical space. In order to achieve this aim, analysts must collate data from users' IP addresses, that locate users within networks and therefore can be used to determine approximate physical location.

Tracking via second party data was recently conducted by Klepers (2020), who assessed online ticketing purchases to trace tourism mobilities. Klepers assessed 140,000 entries of online ticket purchases from 555 events in Latvia. The researcher assessed the origin and destination of festival goers, which allowed them to differentiate local, non-local domestic and international festival goers. Using this technique they were able to assess the impact that different styles of events had upon attracting attendees from different locations. This use of big data (in this case over 1.2 million cleaned entries were used) was very useful as it allowed the research team to go into far more detail than national tourism statistics, as they could assess local travel, non-local but intra-country travel, and also international travel. However, there were some issues with this method – it was not always certain whether the IP address of an event goer at the time of purchase represented their home – ticket purchases could have been made via a hotel concierge, for example, or as a gift from someone not living near the event goers. The researcher also found that 3% of the data was not useable as it had errors such as incomplete IP address. Despite these limitations the authors noted that this method offered great potential for local and regional Destination Management Organisations (DMOs) and researchers to understand visitor flows, as well as forecasting future travel.

10

Conceptual understandings that have emerged from web-based location tracking

Predictors of behaviour

A number of conceptual understandings have emerged from research that has used web-based data to assess tourists' behaviour. One of these is in relation to conversion, which has been tackled on several occasions by academic researchers, to explore whether there is correlation between the country of origin of website visitors and actual arrivals. These studies have confirmed that online search data outperforms nearly all other survey-based indicators in terms of its ability to predict behaviour. Gunter and Önder (2016) used Google Analytics to assess this issue and applied foraging theory to explain search behaviour on DMO's websites. Information foraging has been defined as being a phenomenon whereby:

> '...people will modify their strategies, or modify the structure of the interface if it is malleable, in order to maximize their rate of gaining valuable information. A cognitive strategy will be superior to another if it yields more useful information per unit cost.'
> (Pirolli, & Card, 1999: 646).

According to this theory, the most effective foragers are those who maximise the rate of information they can gather while minimising the cost of gathering this information. Google Analytics data is not available to the public – permission must be gained from the managers of websites to use their Google Analytics data. However, Gunter and Önder (2016) were able to access the data and assess over 20 indicators that Google Analytics uses to assess website usage. This includes data on website users' demographics, interest, online behaviour, the duration that users spend on website, how they found the website, their online engagement, and the bounce rate of the website (percentage of visitors to a website who leave it after viewing only one page). While Google Analytics does not produce data on *actual* spatial movement, the authors were able to use the data on website usage to forecast demand for mobility to destinations in the future. Significantly they found their predictions were more accurate than previously used models that relied on historical visitation statistics. In the COVID-19 era, this is a particularly important issue as the pandemic is an unprecedented event in our modern tourism history and historical data will not suffice as a tool to determine demand.

A further data source that has been used to explore tourist's behaviour is Google Trends. This platform produces two types of data that researchers have been able to use to predict future spatial mobility. The first is real-time data on the most popular Google searches in the last seven days and the second is non-real time data on which searches were popular from 2006 and up to 36 hours before the time of the search (Google, 2020a). Vosen and Schmidt (2011) used Google Trends to forecast short and mid-term tourism demand, and to detect longer-term trends. Their work built upon the work of Fesenmaier et al. (2010), who suggested that search engine data is an essential source for tourism marketers as it reveals which services and attractions are most heavily searched and therefore likely to be considered attractive destinations. They found the platform to be a highly accurate predictor of demand. This finding was supported by Bangwayo-Skeete and Skeete (2015) in later research.

Following this, Volchek et al. (2018) used search query data from Google Trends to undertake further tourism demand forecasting research. Google Trends produces a ratio that illustrates the popularity of search topics at any given point in time across geographical regions or online domains (Höpken et al., 2018). The authors compared Google Trends searches with actual visitation and then applied time series modelling and highly technical artificial neural network models to the data to create forecasts of visitors' arrivals. They concluded that there is definite worth in the use of data such as that from Google – and that different models for forecasting should be chosen depending on the targets that decision makers have – their preference was for the demand forecasting model called SARMAX (seasonal autoregressive moving average with explanatory variables) as they argued it was the most accurate.

Similarly, Höpken, Eberle and Fuchs (2018) assessed web-based search behaviour in order to create forecasts for visitation. The authors assessed patterns of search terms that were used while planning

10

holidays and the relationships that existed between those terms and actual arrivals. They demonstrated that the technique outperformed traditional autoregressive approaches for tourism demand – this traditional approach created predictions based on past arrivals alone.

Figure 10.1: Google's (2020b) data on mobility changes due to COVID-19.

Actual behaviour

Perhaps the most well-known form of tracking spatial mobility via the internet is that which is conducted by Google Mobility. During the COVID crisis, Google released COVID-19 Community Mobility Reports (Google, 2020b). These reports were generated from anonymised data sets of Google users who had enabled their location history setting (thus allowing Google to collate users locations via their IP addresses which give an indication of their location relative to mobile phone towers), and enabled their web activity to be tracked. As the COVID-19 pandemic played out, Google tracked six elements of mobility:

- retail and recreation (including shopping centres, museums, libraries and movie theatres);

- grocery and pharmacy;

- parks;

- transit stations;

- workplace;

- and residential.

Reports were made available for both countries and regions within countries (Figure 10.1). They were designed to give regions and countries insights into the impacts of social distancing and changes in behaviour and movement during the COVID crisis.

In addition to Google associated products, travel review sites have also been used as data sources for understanding patterns of mobility. Trip advisor has become a highly significant travel information source – arguably containing more detail on destinations than DMOs' websites (Xiang and Gretzel, 2010). Van der Zee and Bertocchi (2018) conducted a network analysis on user-generated content from Trip Advisor. They collected their data from over 4,300 profiles via the web scraping software Kimono, and collected data on the users' place of residence, gender, age group and their review from their profile page, plus information on the location of the places that they reviewed. They explored the differences between Belgians, Europeans and non-Europeans and found that while they have distinct review patterns, their behavioural patterns tend to be recurrent. They also found that international

10

reviewers tend to stay close to the tourist hubs – this concurred with the work of Cohen (1972) and Lew and McKercher (2006) who wrote about the existence of tourist bubbles. They found that when visiting a museum that was located out of the major tourist bubble, international reviewers appeared to not use the surrounding restaurants or bars, whereas local reviewers tended to review those places.

The use of bespoke internet-sourced data sets

As well as big data as a source of data for understanding mobility, the internet can also be used to harness smaller data sets. One such data source is travel blogs. These are often meticulously filled out by travellers and detail their movement, itineraries, and travel preferences. Leung, Wang, Wu et al. (2012) used this data source and assessed 500 posts from online trip diaries and blogs between 2001 and 2009: before, during, and after the 2008 Beijing Olympics. They conducted content analysis used with social network analysis software to assess the social networks. The data that they collated allowed them to explore which attractions were visited, especially as the Olympic Games drew closer, along with movement patterns between attractions before and after the Olympics. Their work revealed that while more people came to Beijing as tourists after the Olympics, they still visited the same attractions. They were also able to conceptualise centralisation – the extent to which the network revolves around one of many nodes. This approach to their research showed centralisation decreased after the Olympics, thus suggesting that there was diversification of tourist attractions post-Olympic games. For example, the actual site of the games became a tourist attraction and other subcentres also emerged.

Finally, a promising method for collecting bespoke data sets is the design of mini programs. WeChat released their own mini programs in 2017. These are applications that are embedded within WeChat and do not require downloading or installation. Their popularity has increased rapidly amongst travel enterprises who have gone on to develop their own mini programs (Cheng et al., 2019). Mini programs have many of the functions of apps, but also allow authentication, payment, and communication (Quanzhong, 2017). By 2018, WeChat alone had more than a million mini programs and more than 400 million users (TechWeb, 2018). In Australia, Zhu et al. (2020) have designed a WeChat mini program that tracks tourist's mobility. The researchers are planning to ask tourists to download the app to determine their dispersal when travelling through Australia. This will be one of the first known uses of mini programs designed to assess travel itineraries.

Limitations and ethical issues

Pink et al. (2018), argue that when using digital data, researchers must account fully for the fact that the data may have gaps, or be incomplete. This type of tracking is not without its critics. The primary reason for this is that there are many ethical concerns about this technique and particular caution must be taken to ensure that users of websites are aware that their data is being used to determine their locations. In 2018 Associated Press revealed that Google tracked users locations in two ways – via the Location History function that collected GPS coordinates, and also via a 'Web and App Activity' function that tracked individual's locations (Liao, 2018). Following this revelation, the Australian Competition and Consumer Commission began legal proceedings against Google, claiming that they did not adequately disclose to consumers that two of its settings – Location History and 'Web and App Activity' – were required to be turned off in order to stop location tracking. It was alleged that whilst Google informed its users that Location History should be disabled, they did not clearly inform users of the need to disable the second function – 'Web and App Activity' – in order to cease tracking of location and personal data (Letts, 2019).

Concern over a lack of transparency of the collection of location-based data also extends beyond first-party data, such as that which is collected by Google. The use of third-party data, collected by data aggregator companies, also warrants caution. The European Union's General Data Protection Rule (detailed in Chapter 2) has resulted in a tightening of rules over location-based tracking and requires express consent from users to opt in and share their data. However, further research is still needed to understand whether app users and internet

10

users really understand the extent to which their data is shared. As was highlighted in Chapter 5, Kozinets (2019: 195) noted that:

> *'... a significant number of people – very likely a majority – would prefer that researchers should not use their social media data and information in their investigations.'*

Arguably, this sentiment may also be extended to data pertaining to internet usage as well.

In response to reactions against data usage, plus legislation such as the European Union's General Data Protection Rule, there have been changes. The Google Play store has followed the Android and iOS updates which require apps to give users the choice to opt in to have their location tracked 'while the app is open', 'only once' or 'not at all', and to remind users if they are being tracked.

For researchers who must abide by regional, national and institutional regulations, as outlined in Chapter 2, the ethics of using this data must be considered before beginning a study of this nature. Consideration must be given to the process of data collation, consent, privacy, and the user agreements of the websites that that are being used. Consequently, when data is to be used which has been gained from websites, researchers should consider:

1. The terms and conditions of the website that is being used;

2. The legalities of their research in relation to their country and region where they are located;

3. The ethical requirements of their institution;

4. Whether the users of the websites/app were expressly aware that their data would be used;

5. Whether there was assurance to users of the websites/app that their privacy would be respected.

Conclusion

Tracking tourists' movement via websites can be done in a number of ways. Big data can be sourced via apps such as Google Maps or websites that collate IP numbers and their proximity to mobile phone towers. Big data can also be sourced via big data sets such as ticketing websites that reveal purchase location, or via mini programs such as those used by WeChat. As well as big data, the internet can also be used to collate smaller data sets such as blogs which can be used to determine travel patterns and itineraries.

While tracking movement via websites offers affordable and efficient means by which large amounts of data can be accessed, this form of tracking must treated with caution by researchers. As much of the data has been collected by second or third parties, researchers must ensure that the collation of the data has been done in accordance with ethical standards. This means that researchers must be fully aware of: a) where the data was collected from; and b) that those providing the data (users of websites, apps or mini programs) were fully aware that their data would be used to both track their location and be shared with other parties, such as research institutions. This is not an impossible task by any means, but an essential step that users of this form of data should approach with caution.

Key learnings from this chapter:

- Data that tracks tourists' movement via their internet usage may be collected in a variety of different ways.

- This form of data collection has facilitated accurate insights that can predict tourists' behaviour and track their actual behaviour within destinations

- Data that is sourced via internet usage is non-continuous and so is unable to provide complete tracks of tourists' behaviour.

- This form of data faces significant ethical issues, as consent cannot be gained when collating big data such as this.

10

References

Bangwayo-Skeete, P.F. and Skeete, R.W. (2015) Can Google data improve the forecasting performance of tourist arrivals? A mixed-data sampling approach, *Tourism Management*, **46**, 454–464

Cheng, A., Ren, G., Hong, T., Nam, K. and Koo, C. (2019) An exploratory analysis of travel-related WeChat mini program usage: Affordance Theory perspective, In Pesonen J. and Neidhardt J. (eds), *Information and Communication Technologies in Tourism 2019*, Springer, Cham, pp. 333-343.

Cohen, E. (1972) Toward a sociology of international tourism, *Social Research*, **39**(1), 164–182

Fesenmaier, D.R., Xiang, Z., Pan, B. and Law, R. (2010) An analysis of search engine use for travel planning, In: Gretzel, U., Law, R. and Fuchs, M. (eds.) *Information and Communication Technologies in Tourism*, Springer, New York, pp. 381–392.

Google (2020a) FAQ about Google Trends data, Google Support, Available at: https://support.google.com/trends/answer/4365533?hl=en [Accessed 11 August, 2020]

Google (2020b) COVID-19 Community Mobility Report, Available at: https://www.gstatic.com/covid19/mobility/2020-03-29_AU_Mobility_Report_en.pdf [Accessed 6 June, 2020]

Gunter, U. and Önder, I. (2016) Forecasting city arrivals with Google Analytics, *Annals of Tourism Research*, **61**, 199–212.

Höpken, W., Eberle, T. and Fuchs, M. (2018) Search engine traffic as input for predicting tourist arrivals, *Information and Communication Technologies in Tourism 2018*, Springer, Cham, pp. 381–393.

Klepers, A. (2020) Online ticket purchase as source for tracking tourism mobilities. *Proceedings of the Council of Australasian Tourism and Hospitality Educators Conference 2020 Conference.* Auckland, pp. 21-2.

Kozinets, R. (2019) *Netnography: The Essential Guide to Qualitative Social Media Research*. Third Edition, SAGE Publications.

Letts, S. (2019) Google sued by the ACCC over the alleged misuse of personal data, ABC News, Available at: https://www.abc.net.au/news/2019-10-29/google-faces-accc-federal-court-misleading-use-of-data/11649356 [Accessed 30 October, 2019].

Lew, A. and McKercher, B. (2006) Modeling tourist movements: a local destination analysis, *Annals of Tourism Research*, **33**(2), 403–423

Leung, X. Y., Wang, F., Wu, B., Bai, B., Stahura, K. A. and Xie, Z. (2012) A social network analysis of overseas tourist movement patterns in Beijing: The impact of the Olympic Games, *International Journal of Tourism Research*, **14**(5), 469-484.

Liao, S. (2018) Google still tracks you through the web if you turn off Location History, The Verge, Available at: https://www.theverge.com/2018/8/13/17684660/google-turn-off-location-history-data [Accessed 11 August, 2020]

Mobilewalla (2020) First, second and third-party data: Better together, Available at: https://www.mobilewalla.com/blog/first-second-and-third-party-data-differences [Accessed 11 August, 2020]

Pink, S., Ruckenstein, M., Willim, R. and Duque, M. (2018) Broken data: Conceptualising data in an emerging world, *Big Data & Society*, **5**(1), 1-13.

Pirolli, P. and Card, S. (1999) Information foraging, *Psychological Review,* **106** (4), 643–675.

Quanzhong, G. (2017) Mini program and its future, *News Writ* 3, 28–30

TechWeb (2018), Available at: http://www.techweb.com.cn/data/2018-07-11/2684850.shtml [Accessed 11 August, 2020]

Van der Zee, E. and Bertocchi, D. (2018) Finding patterns in urban tourist behaviour: a social network analysis approach based on TripAdvisor reviews, *Information Technology and Tourism*, **20**, 152-180.

Volchek, K., Liu, A., Song, H. and Buhalis, D. (2018) Forecasting tourist arrivals at attractions: Search engine empowered methodologies, *Tourism Economics, special issue: Tourism Forecasting*, 1-23.

Vosen, S. and Schmidt, T. (2011) Forecasting private consumption: survey-based indicators vs. Google trends, *Journal of Forecasting*, **30**(6), 565–578.

Wills, J. (2020) 7 ways Amazon uses big data to stalk you, Investopedia, Available at: https://www.investopedia.com/articles/insights/090716/7-ways-amazon-uses-big-data-stalk-you-amzn.asp [Accessed 11 August, 2020]

Xiang, Z. and Gretzel, U. (2010) Role of social media in online travel information search. *Tour Management*, **31**(2), 179–188

Zhu, X., Leung A., Lohmann, G. and de Oliveira Santos, G.E. (2020) What do we know about tourist dispersal? A systematic review of literature (1980-2019) Oral presentation at the Council for Australasian Tourism and Hospitality Education 2020 Conference, Auckland, February 2020.

10

11 The Future of Tracking Tourists' Behaviour and Mobility

What this chapter will cover:

- Emergent tracking techniques such as artificial intelligence (AI), machine learning, deep learning and physiological tracking that are likely to further our understandings of tourists' movement and mobility.

- The role that tracking has played during the COVID-19 pandemic.

- The challenges for tourist tracking and innovation in the future.

- A comparative table to guide researchers in selecting the most suitable tourist tracking method.

Introduction

The field of tracking tourists' mobility is a rapidly evolving space. In the eighteen months that it has taken to write this book, many innovations, along with world events such as COVID-19 have emerged, which have required updates to be made to this manuscript. There is no reason to believe that these changes will not continue to be necessary, as technological innovations are likely to occur at a rapid pace and will, no doubt, be utilised by those involved in tourism research.

The purpose of this chapter is to attempt to investigate the future of the adaptations that are likely to occur with regards to tourist tracking technology and methods. A near-future gaze is taken as technology and world events are evolving so quickly that it is difficult to predict a future beyond the short term. Techniques such as physiological tracking, emergency management, indoor positioning, machine learning and artificial intelligence are assessed along with the future of ethical research conduct. A summary is also made where the pros and cons of each research method is assessed and finally, future research needs are highlighted.

Physiological and emotional tracking

Physiological tracking involves combining spatial and temporal data with physiological data. Shoval et al. (2018) ponder whether the use of this form of data in tourism research equates to the introduction of the MRI in medicine, as it offers the potential for new data to emerge and long standing behavioural questions to be answered. Significantly, the technique offers researchers real time data on both emotions and physiological responses to tourism mobility and experiences. This form of data has, until recently, been very scarce within the field of tourism (Shoval et al., 2018) and has tended to focus on emotional responses. One of the reasons why this technique has scarcely been used is that it is onerous in terms of participant requirement, because an experience sampling method (ESM) is commonly used. This was developed in the 1970s and has been used in psychology and psychiatric studies (see Csikszentmihalyi et al., 1977; Csikszentmihalyi and Larson, 1987) and involves the participants self-reporting at intervals, depending on the study. These intervals could be regular (e.g. before during or after an event), predefined intervals, or when signalled by the researcher (Birenboim 2016).

However, technology has decreased the onus on participants to report their emotions. Real-time emotions have been explored by Pettersson and Zillinger (2011) who used geotags on a GPS device and had participants activate a button when they had positive or negative experience. Following this, Birenboim et al. (2015), combined data from

GPS devices with SMS messages to assess real time emotions in the Aalborg Zoo in Denmark, followed by GPS data and a smartphone application at a Students' Day celebration in a large park in Jerusalem that assessed students' momentary experiences, including their sense of crowding and security. Other research has also explored subjective emotions through techniques such as the creation of virtual environments which were then tested via observation, in order to predict visitor movement and emotions such as fatigue, hunger, and boredom (Loiterton and Bishop, 2008).

Technology has also facilitated new explorations into physiological responses to mobility. Kim and Fesenmaier (2015) explored the emotions of tourists using electro-dermal skin sensor technology and were able to uncover strong differences in emotional responses when their participants visited different attractions. Groundbreaking research by Shoval et al. (2018) moved beyond momentary emotions and explored tourists' physiological reactions to travel. This research explored electro-dermal activity (EDA) over time and space and synthesised four data collection methods to assess travellers' mobility alongside their emotions. The methods included:

1. A survey;

2. Tracking data;

3. Real time surveying techniques through experience sampling methods; and

4. Physiological data.

Specifically, the research team used a survey to collect demographic information; a smartphone application that collected GPS and mobile phone network location data; surveys within the app that collected subjective data that was both location-triggered and time-triggered; and physiological measures of emotions, collected via a clinically developed device that measured skin conductance, heart rate measures, blood pressure, and skin temperature simultaneously. This fascinating and multi-dimensional research was able to demonstrate changes over time in tourists' emotional responses. In particular, emotionally evocative areas were able to be determined. The research determined that heightened emotional responses were not confined to the location of

11

tourist sites, but were also evident en route to touristic sites, when they were being viewed for the first time, albeit from a distance.

Given the extreme popularity of wearable technology, there is now great potential for physiological tracking to be integrated with location-based tracking in order to further understand the impacts of tourists' mobility upon tourists' physiological and psychological states. However, what remains to be understood is the impact of the Hawthorne effect and whether the act of tracking impacts upon the tourism experience of participants (Shoval et al., 2018).

Machine learning, AI and predictive modelling

As mentioned in Chapter 1, Schwab (2016) has argued that we are experiencing a fourth industrial revolution, characterized by emerging technologies such as artificial intelligence (AI). Tussyadiah (2020: 2) defines artificial intelligence as "… *a system that thinks humanly, acts humanly, thinks rationally, or acts rationally.*" The fourth era that Schwab argues we are in, places automation along with the ability to make decisions without human involvement using systems such as machine learning (Tussyidiah, 2020). AI offers many possibilities for those wishing to understand tourist mobility. The ability to accurately predict where tourists will travel could have profound impacts upon the way in which the industry operates, as well as the academic research community.

AI is developed by machine learning. This is a process whereby an algorithm is developed from existing data (e.g. previous travel behaviour) that allows the algorithm to predict future behaviour. Machine learning does, from time to time, require engineers to intervene, such as when inaccurate predictions are made. Conversely, deep learning, which has evolved from machine learning and can be considered a subset of the machine learning approach, involves the development of an algorithm, and its own programmed neural network. This means that the algorithm on its own has the capabilities, via its own neural network, to determine if a prediction is accurate or not. As such, deep learning approaches do not require the intervention of humans (Grossfeld, 2020). In recent research, Hardy and Aryal (2020) used a deep learning approach to develop a predictive model of tourist behaviour in Freycinet National Park, Tasmania. Their algorithm was able to predict tourist visitation to single and multiple sites within the Park. As such, AI offers enormous opportunities for the future development of predictive tourism models.

Emergency management

There is an increasing interest in the role that tracking technology can play in assisting authorities to manage tourism and tourists during emergencies (Shoval and Isaacson, 2010). Since 1996 the E911 system has been used in the United States, obligating mobile phone companies to display 911 callers' location to within 50-100 metres. This is the same in Europe where the E112 system is used as 112 is the emergency number in Europe. Under these systems, all calls from mobile phones are directed to call centres that are in the region where the mobile phone is determined to be at the time of the call. The bushfires in Australia over the summer of 2019-2020 utilised a location-based tracking service that allowed text messages to be sent to mobile phones that were detected as being located within fire affected regions. This was particularly important for tourists as the fires occurred during the peak summer holiday season.

There is also the opportunity for apps to track tourists and send push notifications to alert tourists of emergencies. The COVID-19 pandemic has clearly illustrated the potential for this type of technology. The Singaporean app Trace Together (Team TraceTogether, 2020) made use of it to combat community spread of the virus. Its source code was subsequently made open access and has been used by countries such as Australia, and at the time of writing, over 50 countries had expressed interest in using it. The app utilises Bluetooth technology to communicate with other mobile phones that have the app installed. When the app detects another, it uses signal strength indicators vales (RSSI) to measure the signal strength and estimate the distance between users and duration of the encounter. If an app user tests positive for COVID-19 and users are detected to be in range for more than 15 minutes, then the Singaporean Ministry of Health is notified,

11

along with the app user, so that the close contacts can be quarantined, to ensure they do not transmit the disease (Team TraceTogether, 2020). This app has proved useful in contact tracking, although in Australia the Bluetooth functionality has proven difficult with iPhones because the lock-screen function on iPhones disables the Bluetooth functionality, so phones are unable to communicate with each other (Taylor, 2020).

Hype, expectations and plateaus: the future challenges for tracking technology

The rapid uptake of technology and the corresponding proliferation of opportunities to track tourists and understand their behaviour has been met with much excitement, hope and praise from some researchers. At the same time, it has also triggered concern from researchers regarding ethics and data reliability. This phenomena of both optimism and caution to new research methods may be likened to the Gartner Hype Cycle (Gartner, 2020), which outlines fives phases for new technologies (Figure 11.1):

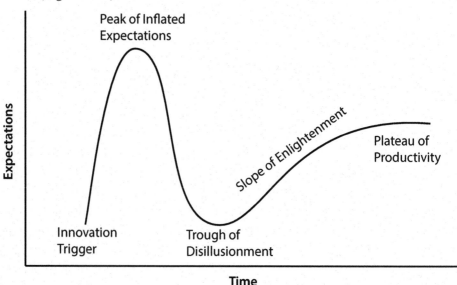

Figure 11.1: The Gartner Hype Cycle (Gartner, 2020).

1. **Technology Trigger** – this is when a new technology is announced that results in media interest, often because it is the first of its type with few alternatives.

2. **Peak of Inflated Expectations** – during this stage, stories of the technology's success, along with many failures, emerge. During this stage early adopters will take up the technology.

3. **Trough of Disillusionment** – this is when interest in the product may wane, and barriers to its implementation arise. In the context of tourism tracking, this is often when issues related to ethics, consent and the reliability of the data have been raised. Those technologies that survive are able to improve their products and satisfy early adopters.

4. **Slope of Enlightenment** – this stage occurs when new iterations of the original technology emerge, its use become more widely used, yet at the same time, those who are more conservative remain cautious of the technology. In the context of tourism research, this is clearly visible as the take up of tracking technologies has arguably been slow – surveys and non-technological solutions to tracking are still ubiquitously used within the research community.

5. **Plateau of Productivity** – during this final stage, the technology is adopted into the mainstream. The use of tourism big data such as consumer sentiment is at this stage, but arguably few if any tourism tracking technologies (with the exception of wearables) have hit the plateau of productivity.

Bringing ethics to the forefront

What has become apparent as new forms of technology and big data have emerged is that ethics and consent remain pivotal issues for those wishing to research the mobility of tourists. The framework for ethical approaches to research, and the requirement for research-ers to consider the context, technological infrastructure, and cultural background of participants, ethical legislation of the research location, and user experience, means that many big data sources that were used when apps and location-based technology was first designed may no

11

longer be considered ethical sources of data. The issues of consent and ethical conduct of research has become even more paramount, given the absence of contact that many tracking researchers may have with individuals whose data they are using.

Looking into the future, it is highly likely that, despite the increasing amount of data being produced on individuals' movement, much of it will be collected with little or no consent, therefore its use for research purposes is questionable at least and unethical at worst. For researchers, consent is arguably the most important issue that they must consider before embarking on this form of research. Consequently it could be argued that is no longer acceptable to take a teleological approach to the use of big data, whereby where the end justifies the means (Hudson, 2007). Rather, a deontological approach, which regards the means as more important than the end should be adopted. Consequently, in the context of big data, individuals and society should be protected when big data is used to track movement.

Not all data is perfect data

What has emerged from the development of this book, as with all forms of data collection, is that there is not one perfect data source. The fact that a data source may be regarded as big data, does not guarantee that the data source is reliable and/or capable of answering research questions. To this end, Pink et al. (2018) wrote that, in order to under- stand digital data, researchers must account fully for the fact the data may have gaps, or be incomplete. Indeed, broken data is a concept that commonly occurs in big and bespoke data sources. This is particularly the case with innovations in tourist tracking data, where repair work is often needed to deal with data gaps or breakages. Interestingly, in the era that we currently live in, where both wearable tracking technol- ogy (e.g. smart watches) and bespoke apps for tracking tourists are now commonly used, we are finding that wearers of technology may become the controllers of their own data. For example, Pink et al. (2018) found behaviours where the wearer purposefully took off their device, such as when they swim. Similarly, the author's experience in the Tourism Tracer research uncovered times where participants disabled the tracking app, either temporarily or permanently. This demonstrates that the assumption that all big or bespoke data produces accurate results should be viewed with caution.

The following table seeks to address the situations where different tracking methods are best used – and avoided (Figure 11.2). Underpinning these options is the ever-present need for ethical research conduct.

Selecting the best method

This book has presented a range of options for researchers to consider when choosing a method to track tourists' mobility. There are many options, each of which contains significant advantages and limitations. Most importantly, the researcher must consider a variety of issues, including:

1. The goals of the research;
2. The ethical implications of the research (an ethical framework was proposed in the first chapter);
3. The ability to gain consent from participants;
4. Budget;
5. Whether continual data is needed;
6. The required accuracy of the data in space and space and time;
7. The length of the study;
8. Where it is being held – indoor or outdoor;
9. The requirement for demographic data along with spatial/ temporal data.

Finally, the researcher should consider the skill set of the team. As was highlighted in this book, each of the suite of methods available requires different skill sets, ranging from app design through to IT skills, GIS analysis skills, and skills in statistical analysis. Tracing tourists mobility requires an interdisciplinary team in order to collate and examine the data and develop theoretical and practical implications. Consequently, the success of this form of research will often be reliant upon the ability of researchers to create teams that can deal

11

these complex sets of data. Figure 11.2 considers many of these issues and assesses the relative strengths and weaknesses of each of the different tracking methods.

Figure 11.2: An assessment of the strengths and weaknesses of differing tracking methods.

Method	Ability to gain consent	Cost per participant of obtaining data	Ability to collect continual and accurate data	Ability to collect accurate spatial data over multiple days	Accuracy of temporal data	Disciplinary expertise required for this method	Location- indoors or outdoors	Ease of syncing location and demographic data
Observation	Possible	High	Med	Low	High	Social science	Both indoors and outdoors	Easily possible
Surveys	Easily possible	Med	Low	Low	Low	Social science	Both indoors and outdoors	Easily possible
GPS	Easily possible	High	Very high	High	High	Spatial science	Outdoors	Easily possible
Social Media	Difficult, onerous	Low	Low	Low	High	Social science + IT	Both indoors and outdoors	Not easily possible
Fitness apps	Possible	Low	Very high	High	High	Social science + spatial science	Outdoors	Possible
Mobile phones towers	Not easily possible	Low	Med	Med	High	IT + social science	Both indoors and outdoors	Possible
Bluetooth	Not easily possible	Low	Med	Low	High	IT + social science	Both indoors and outdoors	Not easily possible
Wi-Fi	Not easily possible	Low	Med	Low	High	IT + social science	Both indoors and outdoors	Not easily possible
Bespoke Apps	Easily possible	Med-High	Very high	High	High	Social science + IT + spatial science	Dependant on technology -can be both indoors and outdoors	Easily possible
Tracking via the internet	Not easily possible	Low	Low	Low	High	IT + social science	Mostly indoors	Medium

Summary

Technology is changing at a very fast pace. In the past ten years, smart technology, wearable technology, artificial intelligence, machine learning, and the introduction of location-based tracking into our smart phones and consequently our everyday lives, has changed the research landscape for those wishing to understand where and how tourists travel. This pace of change is so fast that it is likely that as soon as this book is published, new technologies will have emerged that will be available to tourism researchers.

Despite this, many issues remain the same. The need for tourism researchers to match their research aims with data that answers their research questions will remain. The need for tourism researchers to conduct research that aligns with ethical research standards appropriate to their research jurisdictions will remain. The need for consideration of budgets and staffing skills will also remain as factors that must be considered when selecting a research method. And most importantly, the need to understand that no innovation, technology or method is flawless, will remain. A healthy respect for the opportunities and limitations of each and every research method will ensure that tourist tracking research remains accountable and ethical. This is the most pressing need for tourism research, both now and in the future.

Key learnings from this chapter:

- There are a variety of emergent techniques such as artificial intelligence (AI), machine learning, deep learning and physiological tracking which will further our understandings of tourists' movement and mobility.

- Tracking mobility has played a significant role during the COVID-19 pandemic.

- The COVID-19 pandemic has bought the issue of tracking – and its ethical implications – to the forefront of technological discussions

- Researchers must consider many issues, such as research goals, ethics, budget, style of data needed, accuracy requirements, length and location of study , when selecting the most suitable tourist tracking method.

11

References

Birenboim, A. (2016) New Approaches to the study of tourist experiences in time and space. *Tourism Geographies*, **18**(1), 9–17.

Birenboim A., Reinau, K. H., Shoval, N. and Harder H. (2015) High-resolution measurement and analysis of visitor experiences in time and space: The case of Aalborg Zoo in Denmark, *The Professional Geographer*, **67** (4), 620–9.

Csikszentmihalyi, M. and Larson, R. (1987) Validity and reliability of the experience-sampling method, T*he Journal of Nervous and Mental Disease*, **175**, 526–536.

Csikszentmihalyi, M., Larson, R. and Prescott, S. (1977) The ecology of adolescent activity and experience, *Journal of Youth and Adolescence*, **6**, 281–294.

Gartner (2020) Gartner Hype Cycle, Available at: https://www.gartner.com/en/research/methodologies/gartner-hype-cycle [Accessed 22 June, 2020]

Grossfeld, B. (2020) Deep learning vs machine learning: a simple way to understand the difference, Zendesk, Available at: https://www.zendesk.com/blog/machine-learning-and-deep-learning/ [Accessed 11 August, 2020].

Hardy, A. and Aryal, J. (2020) Using innovations to understand tourist mobility in national parks, *Journal of Sustainable Tourism*, **28**(2), 263-283.

Hudson, S. (2007) To go or not to go? Ethical perspectives on tourism in an 'Outpost of Tyranny', *Journal of Business Ethics*, **76**, 385–396.

Kim, J. J. and Fesenmaier, D. R. (2015) 'Measuring emotions in real time: implications for tourism experience design', *Journal of Travel Research*, **54**(4), 419–29.

Loiterton, D. and Bishop, I. (2008) Simulation, calibration and validation of recreational agents in an urban park environment, In R. Gimblett and H. SkovPetersen (eds), *Monitoring, Simulation, and Management of Visitor Landscapes*, Tuscon, University of Arizona Press, 107–22.

Pettersson, R. and Zillinger, M. (2011) Time and space in event behaviour: Tracking visitors by GPS.' *Tourism Geographies*, **13**(1), 1–20.

Pink, S., Ruckenstein, M., Willim, R. and Duque, M. (2018) Broken data: Conceptualising data in an emerging world, *Big Data & Society*, **5**(1), 1-13.

Schwab, K. (2016) *The Fourth Industrial Revolution*. Geneva: World Economic Forum.

Shoval, N. and Isaacson, M. (2010) *Tourist Mobility and Advanced Tracking Technologies*, New York: Routledge.

Shoval, N., Schvimer, Y. and Tamir, M., (2018) Real-time measurement of tourists' objective and subjective emotions in time and space, *Journal of Travel Research*, **57**(1) 3–16.

Team Trace Together (2020) Available at: https://support.tracetogether.gov.sg/hc/en-sg/categories/360003161013-General, [Accessed 11 August, 2020].

Taylor, J. (2020), Australia's Covidsafe coronavirus tracing app works as few as one in four times for some devices, *The Guardian*, Available at: https://www.theguardian.com/australia-news/2020/jun/17/covid-safe-app-australia-covidsafe-contact-tracing-australian-government-covid19-tracking-problems-working, [Accessed 11 August, 2020].

Tussyadiah, I. (2020) A review of research into automation in tourism: Launching the Annals of Tourism Research curated collection on artificial intelligence and robotics in tourism, *Annals of Tourism Research*, **81**, 1202883.

11

Index